A volume in the series

MASTERS of MODERN LANDSCAPE DESIGN

Library of American Landscape History

RUTH SHELLHORN

KELLY COMRAS

THE UNIVERSITY OF GEORGIA PRESS

ATHENS

LIBRARY OF AMERICAN LANDSCAPE HISTORY

AMHERST

To Mike and Hudson with love

Publication of this book was aided by a generous grant from
Furthermore: a program of the J. M. Kaplan Fund

and by the Bruce and Georgia McEver Fund
for the Arts and Environment.

Published by the University of Georgia Press, Athens, Georgia 30602
www.ugapress.org
in association with Library of American Landscape History

Designed and typeset by Jonathan D. Lippincott
Set in Bembo and Avenir

The paper in this book meets the guidelines for
permanence and durability of the Committee on
Production Guidelines for Book Longevity of the
Council on Library Resources.

Printed in Korea
16 17 18 19 20 P 5 4 3 2 1

Library of Congress Control Number: 2015956060

ISBN 978-0-8203-4963-3

CONTENTS

PREFACE

One of the modern era's most versatile landscape architects, Ruth Shellhorn (1909–2006) designed more than four hundred projects over the course of six decades. Arguably, the most influential of these were the landscape designs she created for Bullock's new department stores—colorful, exotic settings that redefined the suburban shopping experience as a sensuous adventure.

Shellhorn's interest in landscape design was inspired by her Pasadena neighbor the renowned landscape architect Florence Yoch, who created sets for Hollywood films such as *Gone with the Wind*. Yoch encouraged Shellhorn in her career path, but she also warned of the hard work involved, especially for women. In 1927 Shellhorn enrolled in the landscape program at Oregon State College and, after three years, transferred to Cornell University, which offered architectural as well as landscape architectural training. In 1933 she returned to Los Angeles and set up a small residential practice.

Propitious alliances with the region's most talented landscape architects soon led Shellhorn into larger, institutional commissions and increasingly authoritative roles. Her inventive designs were structured by Beaux-Arts principles and enlivened by a sense of modernist abstraction, and her plantings, which utilized both native and exotic species, were planned with an awareness of the region's limited water supply and an eye to sustainability. Shellhorn also collaborated with some of the finest architects in the region, directing construction crews at a time when few women commanded such authority. With a thorough grasp of planning and engineering, she secured many high-profile commissions—from the LA County Shoreline Development Study (1943–44) to Disneyland (1955) and the UC Riverside campus (1956–64). Kelly Comras illuminates the design principles that guided these and other prominent projects as well as several of Shellhorn's private gardens.

Ruth Shellhorn is the first book on this important practitioner and the first volume in the LALH Masters of Modern Landscape Design series. I thank Kelly Comras for bringing the project to LALH and the Viburnum-Trilobum Fund of the New York Community Trust for early support of the series. I am also deeply grateful to Susan L. Klaus and to Furthermore: a program of the J. M. Kaplan Fund.

Sarah Allaback worked closely with the author to develop the manuscript; Mary Bellino copyedited; Derek Gottlieb made the index; Jonathan Lippincott created the series design; and Carol Betsch managed the project in its final stages. Thank you to all of them, to our series advisers, and to our colleagues at the University of Georgia Press.

Robin Karson
Executive Director
Library of American Landscape History

ACKNOWLEDGMENTS

My thanks to Robin Karson, for her faith in me, and Sarah Allaback, an extraordinary editor; Beverly Willis Architecture Foundation; John Randolph Haynes and Dora Haynes Foundation; Charles Birnbaum and The Cultural Landscape Foundation; Genie Guerard and the exceptional staff of UCLA Library Special Collections; Pat Evans; Kathryn Gleason; Steven Keylon; Barbara Lamprecht; Paula Panich; Ann Scheid; David C. Streatfield; Noel Vernon; and Randall Young. The friends, clients, and colleagues of Ruth Shellhorn, as well as her present-day garden owners and a multitude of others, so generous with their time and enthusiasm, are also acknowledged with gratitude. I am most grateful to Mike Lofchie and Hudson Lofchie, and it is to them that this book is dedicated.

RUTH SHELLHORN

OVERVIEW

I was introduced to the work of Ruth Shellhorn in 1968 on a trip with my father to a Bullock's Fashion Square shopping center in Sherman Oaks, California. I remember my wonder at seeing what seemed to be a forest of trees as we pulled into the parking lot. When we stepped out of the car, the scent of pine needles enveloped us, and palm fronds, stirred by the breeze, beckoned us toward the store entrance. After finishing our shopping, we strolled through a parklike plaza, and I admired the espaliered vines spreading across the department store walls. Bold red and yellow flowers nodded on lush hibiscus shrubs. As we sat in the shade of a blooming jacaranda tree, it struck me that this was a special place. I had no idea who created it and did not think to ask. Over a decade would pass before I learned the designer's name.

As a graduate student in landscape architecture at California State Polytechnic University, Pomona, I chose Ruth

Shellhorn, the only woman on my professor's list of important contemporary practitioners, as the subject of a course project. My assignment was to interview Shellhorn, photograph several of her best-known projects, and make a presentation to the class. When we began our interview at the studio behind her home in Redondo Beach, in the South Bay area of Los Angeles County, her reputation was only vaguely familiar to me. But as she spoke, presenting drawings of her work in chronological order, I realized the breadth and significance of her career, as well as the depth of her professional commitment. After the interview, I spent several weekends touring the region, locating as many of her landscape designs as possible. Turning into the Bullock's Fashion Square Sherman Oaks parking lot, I suddenly recalled that remarkable day in my own life. It was then that I understood why Ruth Shellhorn deserved the accolades of her clients, the awards of her peers, and the praise of those who visited her landscapes. Even the uninitiated could recognize something extraordinary in her landscape designs. The experience of being in one of her gardens, so generous and vibrant, will always be with me.

•

Between 1933 and 1990 Ruth Shellhorn created close to four hundred landscape designs, representing a wide range of project types. Her work included award-winning landscape designs for Bullock's department stores and Fashion Square shopping centers, collaboration on the original plan for Disneyland, a multiyear landscape master plan for the University of California at Riverside, a major Los Angeles County coastal planning project, city and regional park designs, and more than two hundred residential estates and gardens. In the course of a nearly sixty-year career, Shellhorn collaborated with some of the most celebrated architects and architectural firms in the region, including Welton Becket; Pereira & Luckman; Skidmore, Owings & Merrill; Killingsworth, Brady & Associates; A. Quincy Jones; and Wallace Neff.

One of the few landscape architects of her day to be born and raised in Southern California, Shellhorn would develop a practice that reflected her lifetime of experience in the region. She witnessed the state's first major efforts to bring in the massive amounts of water necessary to sustain its growing population, the area's increasing development, and the semitropical plants that were used to advertise its promise as a place of comfort, bounty, and opportunity. Water first flowed from the Los Angeles Aqueduct in 1913, and over the next few decades news of the mild California climate and the region's seemingly limitless potential spread across the country. The chance to enjoy outdoor living in one's own tropical paradise became part of the California mystique. An expert on the wide variety of ecologies and microclimates in the southern part of the state, Shellhorn understood how a plentiful water supply could extend the possibilities of landscape design in a semiarid climate. Beginning in the late 1940s, clients, critics, and practitioners praised her work for capturing the essence of Southern California's sun-soaked lifestyle, which they variously described as "the California scene," "the California look," "the California style," "the feeling of early California," and "the spirit of Southern California."[1] As the landscape historian David Streatfield has noted, through her design work and presidency of the Southern California chapter of the American Society of Landscape Architects, Shellhorn would emerge as "one of the leaders in developing [the] regional landscape design idiom."[2]

Although Shellhorn's commercial landscape designs were often identified with the modernist aesthetic, she rejected stylistic ideologies. "I don't have a 'style,'" she once said. "My approach has always been that you have to take that particular site and those particular clients and work with their ideas of what they would like and put it in terms of good design and then adapt it to a site. And if it's a hillside, you have to use the fact that it is a hillside and try not to destroy that." Nonetheless, a sense of classical restraint, proportion, and scale informed her work, which also responded to the needs of urban and suburban clients. As the architectural historian Sam Watters has observed, Shellhorn "negotiated shoals between modernism and traditionalism, reconciling both to succeed as a professional unwilling to cede ground to either ism in the postwar era."[3]

Throughout her career, Shellhorn personally supervised the implementation of her designs and negotiated long-term maintenance contracts with her clients whenever possible. While she understood landscape architecture as a form of art, she also knew that a working sense of the craft was vital to the success of her projects. She conducted much of her own surveying, designed and drafted her own plans, and supervised all construction details, personally checking the operation of each sprinkler head on multiacre projects, for example, before allowing a line to be buried.[4] As consulting landscape architect for Bullock's from 1947 to 1978, she monitored maintenance procedures, visiting sites at least twice a year and following up with reports and recommendations to ensure each landscape's vitality. When pruning, Shellhorn made sketches of individual trees and identified each branch to be removed.[5] This kind of comprehensive vision and understanding of the need for maintenance distinguished her work from that of many other landscape architects of her day, particularly those associated with modernism.[6]

·

Ruth Patricia Shellhorn was born in Los Angeles, California, on September 21, 1909, to Arthur L. Shellhorn, a dentist, and Lodema Gould Shellhorn. She spent her childhood in a quiet neighborhood in South Pasadena. With her father, Ruth enjoyed weeklong camping trips to the High Sierras and Sunday drives to see the spring wildflowers in the desert, sharing his passion for solitude in nature (fig. 1). Her mother managed a paternal inheritance with investments in real estate and utilities, led several community organizations, and served as the civic beautification chairman for the Los Angeles Chamber of Commerce. Both parents were college graduates who valued education and were progressive enough to invest in a higher education for their daughter. They encouraged Ruth's interest in art as a child, and they also encouraged the development of her natural mathematical abilities.[7] She grew up believing that, with perseverance, she could take on any career she chose. At a time when most of her friends were contemplating marriage and children, Ruth began considering her life's work.

Counseled by her neighbor, the landscape architect Florence Yoch, Shellhorn, at age fifteen, decided to pursue a career in landscape architecture. "[Yoch] discouraged me by saying that I had to have four years of Latin, chemistry, etc., must be dedicated to hard work, and not think of landscape architecture as pure pleasure. The more I thought about what she said, after my initial discouragement, the more I was determined to show her that I had what it took to be a landscape architect."[8] As if she understood the importance of her decision, Shellhorn began recording her thoughts in a

Figure 1. Ruth and Arthur Shellhorn on a family outing, c. 1913. Photograph by Lodema Shellhorn. In the author's possession.

personal diary, a habit she would continue, almost daily, for the rest of her life.

In the fall of 1927, Shellhorn enrolled in the School of Landscape Architecture at Oregon State Agricultural College (now Oregon State University) in Corvallis (fig. 2). An outstanding student, she was the first woman to win the Alpha Zeta Scholarship Cup for the highest marks in the School of Agriculture and was also awarded the Clara Waldo Prize for Most Outstanding Freshman Woman. She was named to the Phi Kappa Phi honor society in her junior year and earned a national class prize in a Beaux-Arts design competition.[9] As her senior year approached, Shellhorn realized she would need professional training in architecture to more fully develop her command of spatial composition. In spite of the devastating effects of the stock market crash, her family found the resources for her to transfer to Cornell University in 1930.[10]

When Shellhorn arrived at Cornell, the School of Land-

Figure 2. Shellhorn with fellow student in drafting studio at Oregon State, c. 1930. In the author's possession.

scape Architecture was among the best in the country. Founded in 1904, its pedagogy followed the atelier model and educational approach of the École des Beaux-Arts, with significant results. The decade before Shellhorn began her studies, Cornell students won the first three Rome Prize Fellowships, offered by the American Academy in Rome, in landscape architecture.[11] At Cornell, Shellhorn excelled in her studies and again distinguished herself with honors for her design work and service to the academic community. She won a competition with an exquisite illustration of a sixteenth-century English estate, which still hangs in Sibley Hall (fig. 3). With an architecture student, George Bottcher, she shared the Charles Goodwin Sands Memorial Medal for the most outstanding design in a collaborative senior project, a "Summer White House." She also served as president of the Psi chapter of Kappa Kappa Gamma in 1930–31 and was named consulting national architect for the sorority from 1931 to 1936, taking the position back home with her when she left Cornell in 1933. This post, although unpaid, enabled Shellhorn to become familiar with architectural practices in a professional setting and gave her experience in managing the work of others at an early stage in her career.[12]

Since 1904, when it was called the Outdoor Program, female students had matriculated in landscape architecture at Cornell but were rarely treated as the equals of their male counterparts. The administration perceived women as less able to find work in the profession, a prejudice reinforced by the Depression-era belief that men who supported families should have priority over women in the race to obtain scarce jobs.[13]

By the 1930s, Cornell had only just begun to engage in the excitement surrounding the modern movement. Emerging out of Europe after World War I, the new design aesthetic introduced Americans to bold ideas about form and function in architecture that promised a better way of life. The Harvard Graduate School of Design led East Coast academia in embracing modernist design principles at a time

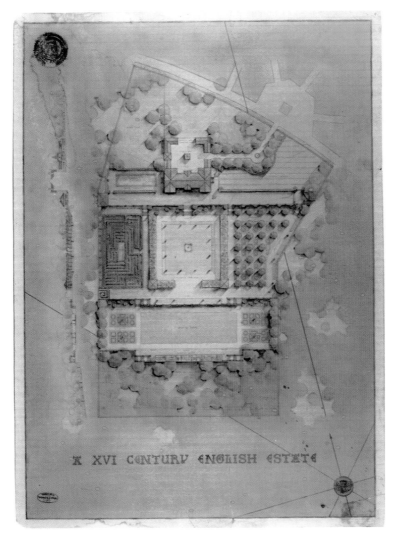

Figure 3. Shellhorn's design for "A XVI Century English Estate," c. 1932.
Courtesy Cornell University.

when "hardly a ripple of controversy" was noticed at Cornell.[14] Despite the faculty's conservative position, Shellhorn was aware of the shifting ground; she shared drafting studio space with architecture students who were experimenting with the International Style, and she found the new ideas exhilarating (fig. 4). She took a course on city and regional planning that captivated her, inspiring a life-long interest, and she attended lectures in the architecture program, such as Egerton Swartwout's "The Trend in Modern Architecture."[15] She made notes about these lectures in her diary, observing, for example, that "rooms should be designed and distributed properly to make the building—rather than making a building and then fitting rooms into it."[16]

Along with her fellow landscape architecture students, Shellhorn began exploring the application of modernist ideas, primarily the interrelationship between interior and

Figure 4. Landscape architecture and architecture students at Cornell University, c. 1932. In the author's possession.

exterior space. She studied current periodicals, including *Landscape Architecture,* where Fletcher Steele published "New Pioneering in Garden Design," one of the earliest discussions of modern landscape design, and the exhibition catalog *Contemporary American Sculpture,* which showcased modern art forms in the landscape.[17] Her library reflected her wide-ranging interests and eclectic tastes. Among her books were *Steel Construction: A Manual for Architects, Engineers and Fabricators of Buildings and Other Steel Structures* (1932), Edith Wharton's *Italian Villas and Their Gardens* (1904), John F. Harbeson's *The Study of Architectural Design* (1927), and *How France Built Her Cathedrals: A Study in the Twelfth and Thirteenth Centuries,* by Elizabeth Boyle O'Reilly (1921). Although she went on to experiment with many elements of modernist landscape design, she never identified with any particular stylistic camp, a reflection, perhaps, of her inner authority.

In 1933, after completing six years of school, Shellhorn found herself four units short of her degree but unable to afford the tuition for an additional semester. Her dean refused to let her double up her course load because he believed women did not have the physical stamina for such an undertaking, and, as a result, Shellhorn left Cornell without a degree. But her determination to continue her education persevered. Before returning home in the spring of 1933, she visited the "Century of Progress" World's Fair in Chicago, an experience that introduced her to new forms, materials, and methods of construction.

Rather than take the train back to Los Angeles, Shellhorn purchased a berth on a mail steamer traveling through the Panama Canal and began a three-week trip that included stops in the Caribbean and Central America (fig. 5). In her journal, she recorded her observations of the islands, ports, local architecture, gardens, and flora. The layout of town squares, churches, and marketplaces also captured her interest, and she took careful notes on the design and use of these public spaces. After visiting the walled city and fort in Cartagena, Colombia, she observed how efficiently the space connected the churches and civic buildings. She delighted in the geometry of the house gardens, public court-

Figure 5. Passenger list for the steamship *Santa Cecilia*, June 1933. Ruth Shellhorn Papers, Library Special Collections, Charles E. Young Research Library, UCLA (RSP).

yards, pebbled-concrete walkways, and tile work. The San Pedro Claver Church and Convent in Cartagena, which featured thick walls of varying height and textured bricks, and the street fronted with colorful tiled walls and overhanging balconies of delicate grillwork, left lasting impressions. She wrote evocatively about the "brilliant green foliage—waves breaking on the rocky shore"; the warm nights in Haiti, the "air soft and moist" with the "smell of wet palm leaves, tropical flowers, seaweed and smoke from the wood fires" and the "sea like indigo and smooth as if oiled."[18] She also filled her journal with notes about the botanical bounty of the region; hibiscus, bougainvillea, crepe myrtle, flowering almond, rubber trees, and numerous species of palm trees would subsequently find their way into her planting plans (fig. 6). Shellhorn's journal also included pages of description about the construction and operation of the Panama Canal locks. Her notes on the precise size and weight of the lock

Figure 6. The port of Cristóbal, in the Panamanian province of Colón, 1933. Photographer unknown. In the author's possession.

doors suggest an interest in engineering that would become apparent in her design of construction details. She may have profited more from her solitary three-week journey through the Caribbean and Panama than from the typical tour of Europe enjoyed by many of her peers.

By the time Shellhorn reached Los Angeles in June 1933, Roosevelt had begun to enact his New Deal programs, intended in part to counter massive unemployment. For landscape architects across the country, the establishment of the Works Progress Administration in 1935 offered new hope, as many found jobs working in national, state, and regional parks. Major public projects, such as the construction of Hoover Dam, renewed Americans' faith in economic recovery. Within weeks of Shellhorn's return, Wiley Post successfully completed the first solo flight around the world. An era of great promise had begun.

Despite the potential for finding design work in Los Angeles, job opportunities for female landscape architects were rare. Shellhorn, however, would benefit from the elite education that distinguished her from many of the male practitioners in Southern California who had established themselves through apprenticeships in the design departments of nurseries in the 1920s and 1930s, as well as from most female practitioners who were either self-taught, mentored, or had studied landscape architecture only briefly.[19] Her progressive upbringing was an additional asset, as was her persistence. Even after being rejected for New Deal government positions, she pressed on. "I think a lot of it's in your own attitude," she said later. "If you go at it as a person, you're not a woman or a man. It doesn't make any difference. You have a problem to solve. So you cooperate and you work on that problem."[20]

Shellhorn had hoped to work for Florence Yoch after finishing her education, but the landscape architect was only able to offer her a few brief drafting assignments. (Yoch's partnership with Lucile Council between 1925 and 1964 focused on residential and smaller commercial projects.)[21] Yoch did offer Shellhorn priceless advice, however, counseling her to pay meticulous attention to the details of design, focus on the craftsmanship of construction, exert absolute control over a project whenever possible, and insist on long-term maintenance to extend the initial integrity of the landscapes. "Otherwise," Yoch insisted, "the gardens fall apart." Over time, these imperatives became trademarks of Shellhorn's practice.[22]

On returning home, Shellhorn discovered that Southern California had become a creative center of horticultural research and offered invaluable resources for landscape architects. While searching for work, she had ample opportunity to visit some of the nation's outstanding botanical collections, such as the Huntington and later Descano Gardens, and to study exotic and newly hybridized plants (fig. 7). She attended lectures, patronized private growers and hybridizers, and eventually developed relationships with owners of nurseries involved in introducing new species and cultivars, including Evans & Reeves in Brentwood.[23] The Pasadena area also gathered formidable intellectual talent in scientific research, the fine arts, music, and literature. Einstein was in his third winter of residence at the California Institute of Technology, and the city was host to the oldest chamber music society in the nation. Shellhorn regularly attended the Playbox Theater, which produced a number of critically acclaimed experimental plays.

After her experience at Cornell, Shellhorn looked at her surroundings with a renewed appreciation for regional architecture. Between 1903 and 1912, Henry and Charles Greene had produced some of the finest examples of the bungalow, derived from the English Arts and Crafts movement and

Figure 7. Japanese Garden, Huntington Library, 1932. Photograph by Ralph
Cornell. Courtesy Ralph D. Cornell papers (Collection 1411), Library Special Collections, Charles E. Young
Research Library, UCLA.

adapted to Southern California. Shellhorn was familiar with
the Greenes' work, which featured wide eaves, broad porches,
sheltered sleeping porches, and gardens functioning as outdoor rooms. Near her childhood home in Pasadena, Irving
Gill's 1911 Miltmore House incorporated what Gill called his
"green rooms," broad covered porches opening out into the
gardens that served as entranceways and patios.[24] Local architects also employed the Spanish Colonial Revival style, which
typically included enclosed gardens accompanied by patios,
trellis-work roofs, and covered walkways. In the 1920s, the
architect Wallace Neff created some of the finest examples of
French Norman, Italian, and Spanish Revival in the area.[25]

In her effort to find work, Shellhorn looked for new ways

to expand her social network and meet fellow practitioners. Through family friends, she met Katherine Bashford, an established landscape architect who not only encouraged her to become part of the local chapter of the American Society of Landscape Architects but introduced her to ASLA members and included her in the society's activities.[26] Bashford was making her mark in the 1930s by designing single-family residential gardens, public landscapes, and campuses that were praised for balancing historical classical details with a Mediterranean plant palette, all the while maintaining a spirit of regionalism.[27] During this time, Shellhorn also met Beatrix Farrand, one of the most successful American landscape architects of her generation. The only woman among eleven founding members of ASLA in 1899, Farrand had moved to Pasadena when her husband, Max Farrand, became the director of the Huntington Library. She joined the local ASLA chapter in 1927 and the next year designed a landscape plan for the Hale Solar Laboratory. She went on to create a campus plan for the California Institute of Technology (1928–1938) and a significant redesign of the campus at Occidental College in Los Angeles (1936–1941).[28] Bashford and Farrand were part of a strong tradition of women landscape designers in the United States, and Shellhorn's exposure to their diverse practices undoubtedly expanded her perspective on professional opportunities in the field.[29]

Although she attributed her most successful projects to following Yoch's advice on the importance of maintenance review and looked to Farrand as an exemplar of style, Ralph Dalton Cornell would exert still greater influence on Shellhorn's professional development. In February 1934 she went to Cornell's office seeking employment. Nineteen years older than Shellhorn and with a graduate degree from Harvard in landscape architecture, Cornell had recently ended a decade-long partnership with Cook, Hall & Cornell. His practice included an impressive body of residential work, as well as public works, subdivisions, and community planning. A close friend and former business partner of the native plant horticulturist Theodore Payne, Cornell was a consummate plantsman in his own right. His book *Conspicuous California Plants, with Notes on Their Garden Uses,* published in 1938, became a valued reference for California landscape architects. Although unable to offer Shellhorn any work, Cornell was impressed by her educational credentials and began a professional friendship with the ambitious young landscape architect. His initial advice to Shellhorn was to set up her own office and seek out her own clients.[30]

Cornell's counsel and support then and over the course of her career encouraged Shellhorn to achieve professional independence. Under his tutelage, she abandoned what she later called "fussy" annual flowering plant palettes and learned to develop the bold, structural planting arrangements that characterized her mature work. He taught her to plant for simplicity, durability, and longevity—promoting the use of native plants and the philosophy behind what are now known as sustainable landscapes. He also shared his enthusiasm for the rapidly expanding field of urban planning. The man she called "Mr. Cornell" and the landscape architect with talent and gumption whom he called "Rufus" remained friends until Cornell's death in 1972.[31]

During the Great Depression, Shellhorn was able to establish a small residential practice, completing a number of commissions for private gardens before the outbreak of World War II. In early 1934 she displayed examples of her landscape drawings in a design show at Barker Brothers, a home furnishings store.[32] There she met Katherine Musselwhite, an interior decorator, and the architect Frank W.

Green. The three young designers created an impromptu partnership to provide a package of services for a residential client in Whittier, a suburb southeast of Los Angeles. Over the next decade Shellhorn designed ten residential gardens in the Whittier neighborhood, at least two with Green.[33] Her relationship with Green and Musselwhite set a pattern that was to recur throughout her career: after a collaborative project, many colleagues would not only recommend her for other jobs, but also hire her to create landscape designs for their own homes and businesses.[34]

During the summer of 1935 Shellhorn began her first nonresidential project—a landscape design for South Pasadena High School, her alma mater. She was responsible to the school board for the design and construction of all phases of the work. The three-year project included a design for a main quadrangle flanked by two buildings, an enclosed courtyard, and an athletic field. The plans demonstrate her sensitivity to domestic scale, appreciation for the relationship between indoor and outdoor spaces, and consideration of function as well as beauty.

In January 1936 Shellhorn and her mother visited the architect Richard Neutra, who had emigrated from Germany with his wife, Dione, in the early 1920s. The ostensible reason for the Shellhorns' visit was to hear Dione, an accomplished singer and cellist, perform, but Ruth was invited to come back and show Neutra some of her plans. He may have been considering her for his upcoming entry in the California House and Garden exhibition in Los Angeles, but this commission went to Ralph Cornell, who immediately offered Shellhorn the opportunity to work on the plan in his office.[35] In response to Neutra's spare design, Shellhorn created a planting scheme of fine-textured plants—a broad panel of tightly clipped lawn and a bed of evergreen shrubs with small, feathery leaves—that served as a counterpoint to the simplicity of the building.

That spring, Shellhorn continued her efforts to further her education and professional development. Having long dreamed of a trip to Europe, she conceived of a plan to pay

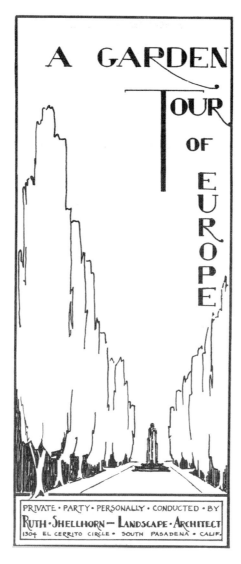

Figure 8. Shellhorn's European garden tour brochure, 1936. In the author's possession.

her expenses by leading Cornell University students on a group tour of European gardens and went so far as to arrange a schedule and design a brochure (fig. 8).[36] Although eventually forced to abandon the project, Shellhorn found other opportunities to expand her professional horizons through her connection with Ralph Cornell, who had consistently encouraged her to pursue ASLA membership. In July 1936 she joined the organization as a junior member, a decision she would look back on as a turning point in her career. She soon took advantage of the opportunity to strengthen her professional relationships by working on the chapter's monthly newsletter and helping with professional outreach.

Throughout the late 1930s, Shellhorn pursued every possible opportunity to display her work and obtain commissions. She gave a talk at the 1937 California House and Garden exhibition in Los Angeles, which included her landscape design for an "Economy House."[37] Her collaboration with Frank Green on the H. P. Larkin residence and garden (1935), one of thirty winners in the architect's competition, was published in *House and Garden*.[38] At one of his dinner parties, Cornell introduced her to a *Sunset Magazine* editor, which resulted in her being invited to write a short article on flower shows for the April 1938 issue.[39] That summer, she exhibited a watercolor and photographs of a garden she had designed in 1935–36 for a local banker, L. H. Jenkins, in an ASLA exhibit at the Los Angeles County Fair (fig. 9).[40] She also received publicity for residential landscape designs for the architect William H. Harrison, published in the California-based journal *Architect and Engineer,* and two residential gardens for the architect Arthur R. Hutchason, one of which was featured in the *House and Garden* architects' competition in 1937 and subsequently published in *California Arts and Architecture* magazine.[41] These early plans gave little hint of the

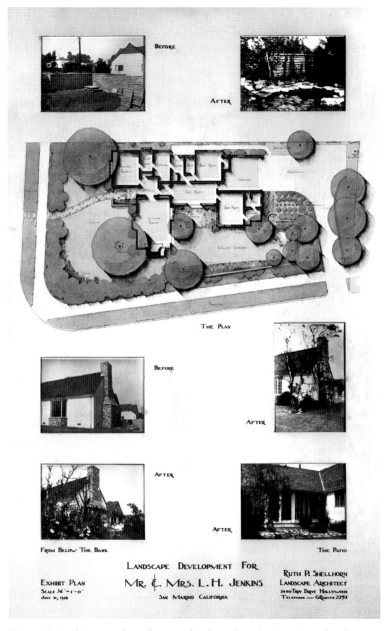

Figure 9. Jenkins garden plan, as displayed at the Los Angeles County Fair's ASLA exhibit, 1938. In the author's possession.

24   RUTH SHELLHORN

originality of her later work, but among her drawings of this time was a 1938 design for Rose McLaughlin's three-acre hillside house and garden in North Hollywood, sensitively sited near a wooded area and accommodating an adjacent stream, a suggestion of her emerging, unique style.

By 1939 Shellhorn found herself working six and even seven days a week, but still struggling with the expense of running her new business. In May she showed some of her drawings to Roland E. Coate, a prominent Pasadena architect. Coate was a graduate of Cornell University (he completed his degree in 1914), and she hoped their affiliation might bring her some work. Shellhorn and Coate apparently did not like each other at first (she called him an "old poker face" in her diary), but almost a decade later he offered her employment on a residence for Edith Knapp.[42] Coate was impressed by her resolution of the Knapp property's spatial constraints and her knowledge of a wide range of plants. Shellhorn was pleased with the results she achieved in the Knapp garden, several images of which were published in *Sunset Magazine*. She and Coate would work together on three additional residential projects during the 1950s, and Coate also consulted with her on a plan for his own garden. When recommending Shellhorn, he assured his clients, "You couldn't do better."[43]

In the fall of 1939, Shellhorn accepted an offer from *Sunset Magazine* to write and illustrate a series of seven articles.[44] Her essays focused on solutions to typical garden design problems encountered by suburban homeowners, many of which she had resolved in a landscape she had designed for Gardener and Elizabeth Grout in Pasadena the year before (fig. 10). Recalling this commission, in the first article of the series she described the importance of early planning, noting that "to attempt a garden without it means failure even

Figure 10. Shellhorn supervising the installation of an oak tree in the Grout garden, 1939. Photograph by Arthur Shellhorn. In the author's possession.

before you've planted the first shrub," and she encouraged clients to think of their home and garden as a single, unified whole, with "a natural flow from house to garden, just as there is from one room to another."[45] Later articles focused on the best method of organizing space to accommodate specific activities, such as outdoor games or gardening, the need to establish the center of interest in a garden, the importance of screening and enclosing spaces on small properties, and the value of visual balance in landscape composition. The articles were clearly written, distilling useful design principles into a simple format that introduced each in terms of the "right way" and "wrong way" of achieving the desired result. The assignment gave her some welcome publicity and the opportunity to describe her evolving principles of design to an audience of potential clients.

In March 1940, as Shellhorn was completing the final *Sunset* article, Cornell, Bashford, and fellow landscape architect Tommy Tomson sponsored her for full membership in

ASLA. Along with their recommendations, her application portfolio included the *Sunset Magazine* articles as well as plans, photographs, and notes for the Grout, McLaughlin, Jenkins, and South Pasadena High School landscape designs.[46]

Shellhorn had always assumed she would marry and have children, but in 1940, at age thirty-one, she was still single and living with her parents. By the time she met Harry A. Kueser she had discouraged several suitors because she feared that marriage would require giving up her work. Kueser presented a different arrangement. Eleven years older and working as a mid-level bank manager, he supported her professional aspirations.[47] They married on November 21, 1940, and settled into a life of separate careers and weekend driving trips. All of her girlhood friends, as well as her family members, were shocked when she continued to practice, although she did relocate her office from Hollywood to her home in South Pasadena a year later (fig. 11). At the time,

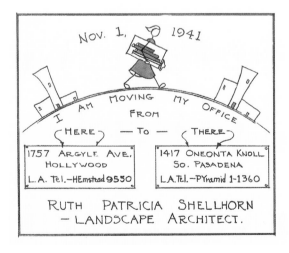

Figure 11. Shellhorn's announcement of her move to a home studio, 1941. In the author's possession.

her marriage was considered unconventional by most definitions, but her personal view of what was possible would appear more realistic as World War II helped bring about alternative scripts for womanhood.

By the end of 1941, with the country officially engaged in war, finding work in landscape architecture had become increasingly challenging. Shellhorn's most promising project, an estate design for Ben Goetz, an MGM movie studio executive, in Pacific Palisades, was halted before its completion. Very few residential garden commissions were available, and the development of public projects took second priority to the war effort. Later, Shellhorn recalled that even experienced landscape architects were struggling to find employment during wartime. Florence Yoch briefly worked on aerial surveys, Edward Huntsman-Trout and the architect H. Roy Kelley camouflaged an aircraft factory with a cloth printed with houses, streets, and landscapes, and Ralph Cornell focused on war-related housing and design projects, while Katherine Bashford, George Hall, and Wilbur D. Cook Jr. retired.[48]

In spite of the scarcity of work, Cornell invited Shellhorn to become his associate in September 1942.[49] Perhaps recalling Yoch's advice, she declined the offer, determined to pursue her goal of exerting complete control over her own output from conception to completion. Remarkably, Shellhorn's prospects improved during this difficult time. In 1943 she was hired to help create a regional landscape restoration and recreation plan for an eleven-mile stretch of coast in Los Angeles County. The Shoreline Development Study was funded by a private group of businessmen, the Greater Los Angeles Citizens Committee, and provided an extraordinary opportunity for planners to shape the future of the Southern California coastline. The plan included park designs for the cities of Manhattan Beach and Torrance and a regional park for Redondo Beach and Hermosa Beach (fig. 12). The Shoreline Development Study's long-term recommendations included restrictions on oil drilling in Santa Monica Bay and presaged the implementation of the Cali-

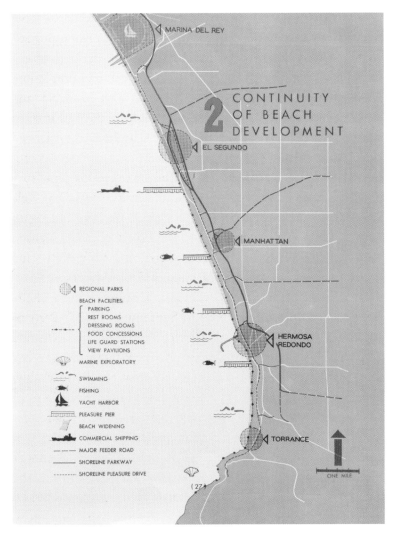

Figure 12. *Shoreline Development Study,* beach development plan, 1944. In the author's possession.

fornia Coastal Act of 1976, a significant environmental protection measure.

The Shoreline Development Study was a professional breakthrough for Shellhorn, both as an opportunity to delve deeply into the then relatively unstructured process of regional park planning and as a means of establishing the network of contacts that would lead to her future success. Carl McElvy, who would later become the state architect for California, supervised her work. McElvy immediately recognized her talent for evaluating spatial and aesthetic issues and appreciated her intelligence. He taught her how to appraise a site and analyze the different programmatic requirements and physical circumstances of each community in the project. He also showed her how to seek out land purchase opportunities by checking the tax and ownership status of proposed park properties. P. G. Winnett, the Citizens Committee's president and the president of Bullock's Department Stores, had also taken notice of Shellhorn's role in the project.

After the publication of the Shoreline Development Study in 1944, Shellhorn undertook several private garden designs and developed a general site plan for a park in the desert city of Indio, California. During this time, she often worked on her own projects at night and spent days working with Cornell on Glen Haven Memorial Park in northern Los Angeles and a shopping center in nearby Lakewood, among other projects. He repeated his offer of a partnership in September 1944, but she declined again, believing the arrangement would hold her back because she "had what it took to make it on her own."[50] She was rightly optimistic. Carl McElvy, her supervisor on the Shoreline Study, landed the commission for Bullock's Pasadena just a few weeks later and, with P. G. Winnett's full support, he asked Shellhorn to be his site planner and associate. The position would not begin for more than a year, but this timing worked well for Shellhorn, who was juggling work with Cornell and a full-time practice of her own. The stakes for success were rising, too, because Kueser had impulsively resigned after twenty years with Bank of America, leaving her as the couple's breadwinner.[51]

With the Bullock's Pasadena project on the drawing board and an increasing number of residential commissions entering her office throughout 1945, Shellhorn found herself restructuring her work process. She hired contractors to install many of her designs. By the end of the war, she realized the critical importance of including features that enhanced outdoor living, such as barbecues and pergolas, and routinely included them. Kueser took on a supervisory role, and the couple soon found that they seldom worked fewer than six days a week. During this busy time, Cornell offered her two important large-scale public projects: the designs for Verdugo Park in Glendale (fig. 13) and Centinela Park in Inglewood. Although she completed the plans in his office as his employee, Cornell

Figure 13. Verdugo Park, Glendale, 1944. Courtesy RSP.

continued to demonstrate his support by allowing her to include her name on the plans as the landscape architect.[52] He asked her once again to consider an association with him, but by now she was determined to head out on her own.

•

As the country began its recovery from economic depression and war, Shellhorn became increasingly active in the Southern California chapter of ASLA, and in November 1945 she was elected its president. She would lead the chapter from January1946 to the end of 1948—three years that marked an unprecedented opportunity to shape new landscape paradigms for the postwar epoch. Membership in ASLA provided the only means of establishing professional credibility until state licensure was implemented in 1954. Shellhorn's tenure as president overlapped with a sharp rise in ASLA membership and a move toward professionalization. She helped push forward a determined effort by ASLA's national committee on professional registration to further the cause of landscape architects in their fight for state registration and licensure. She planned meetings and letter-writing campaigns that eventually led to successful legislation in California, the first state to take this step.[53]

Having recently completed the coastal development project and two public parks, Shellhorn was confident in her knowledge of regional planning issues, and she used her authority as chapter president to emphasize the importance of regional planning. She devoted a third of the ASLA meetings to planning projects, including those of the Los Angeles County Department of Parks and Recreation and the Los Angeles Planning Department.[54] Shellhorn began to significantly enlarge the chapter's scope of inquiry at the same time that planning, zoning, housing, and environmental regulation were gaining prominence in shaping the urban and suburban landscape.

Throughout her ASLA chapter presidency, Shellhorn initiated a significant exchange of ideas about the expanding professional role, social purpose, and process of landscape design. She organized frequent lectures and field trips to learn about the ongoing work of members and associated professionals, including planners and nursery specialists. In May 1946 Ralph Cornell showed slides of his recent projects, and members visited sites ranging from the Caltech campus to the local specialty nursery Millikan Iris Gardens. In June, members toured Tommy Tomson's landscape design for Park la Brea, a 175-acre garden apartment development built by the Metropolitan Life Insurance Company, and Cornell and Edward Huntsman-Trout led a tour through the Pomona and Scripps College campuses.[55] That October, Lockwood de Forest Jr. hosted a weekend trip to Santa Barbara to see some of his residential gardens. At year's end, chapter members, led by Fred Barlow Jr., began planning for the first annual national conference in California, to be held in Ojai in 1950 (fig. 14), and Carl McElvy handed his commissions for Bullock's Pasadena and Palm Springs to Shellhorn when his workload got too full.

Shellhorn organized an equally full slate of ASLA activities in 1947, focusing on the work of practitioners she respected, significant environmental issues, and innovative new designs, including her own. Ralph Cornell reported on the new master plan for the California Arboretum in Santa Anita, a project that many members actively sponsored. A February meeting elicited support for the San Gorgonio Primitive Area (now the San Gorgonio Wilderness) in the San Bernardino National Forest. Shellhorn invited the San Francisco–based landscape architect Thomas Church and his

Figure 14. Southern California chapter of ASLA, first annual meeting at the Ojai Valley Inn, 1950. Shellhorn in middle row, tenth from right. Courtesy RSP.

wife to the May meeting, which included a tour of six gardens in Bel-Air designed by Art Barton.

In mid-September Shellhorn led a tour of her interior courtyard design for the First Methodist Church in Pasadena and her newly completed landscape design for Bullock's Pasadena (fig. 15). The first modern department store in the region to be located in the suburbs and one of the first to explicitly accommodate the automobile, Bullock's Pasadena was a bellwether for the industry. The company's president, P. G. Winnett, envisioned a series of his stores in suburban locations that would appeal to America's growing upper middle class. An immediate success, Bullock's Pasadena garnered Shellhorn her first Los Angeles Beautiful award and attracted crowds of eager shoppers. Her innovative plantings captured the admiration of her colleagues, including de Forest, who later wrote to her, "I saw it one night last fall and thought it was the best planting that I had seen. I liked everything about it, your combination of texture, your use of interesting material . . . I am rushing around telling everyone."[56]

Shellhorn's breakthrough in her Bullock's landscapes was propelled by the realization that shopping was a leisure activity. Her designs would define shopping in the open air as a pleasurable experience, even an adventure. Company executives strove to tempt middle-class disposable income to their stores by placing strong emphasis on the individual shopper's experience; the customer was "first of all, a guest."[57] The Bullock's mission fit well with Shellhorn's own philosophical approach toward the design of public space. She believed that the best design for groups of people addressed them as individuals, not members of the "faceless masses."[58] She aimed for the attention and satisfaction of women—specifically, the woman of the house who held upwardly mobile aspirations. The Bullock's landscape was thus designed to entice the energetic housewife to spend an extended period of time shopping, invite the weary shopper to linger, and induce the man of the house to willingly wait for his wife while she shopped. Shellhorn accomplished this ambitious goal by infringing on

Figure 15. Bullock's Pasadena facing Lake Avenue, 1967. Photographer unknown. In the author's possession.

some of the retailer's standard means of maximizing commercial success. She advocated for a spaciousness not usually tolerated in retail design, creating pedestrian oases within the overall landscape and paying close attention to planting and construction details, all of which might remind shoppers

Figure 16. Bullock's Wilshire, stairwell atrium planting, 1952. Photograph by Douglas M. Simmonds. In the author's possession.

of the more intimate, inviting gardens of a gracious home. By creating such relaxing settings, Shellhorn set the standard for the shopping mall of future generations. In the process, her Bullock's designs became icons of the Southern California landscape (figs. 16 and 17).

Figure 17. Bullock's Wilshire, parking court entrance, 1952. Photograph by Douglas M. Simmonds. In the author's possession.

The public response to Shellhorn's plans thrilled Winnett. In return, she appreciated working for an enlightened client who shared her vision of modern, elegant design and was prepared to invest the resources necessary to implement and maintain her projects. The bond that developed between Bullock's management and Shellhorn became so strong that when she was underbid on her proposal to design the landscape for Bullock's Westwood in 1950, Winnett intervened to alter established corporate bidding policy and assure her

Figure 18. Mahlon Arnett, Bullock's president, and architect MacDonald Becket (son and business partner of Welton Becket) with model of Bullock's Fashion Square Del Amo, 1964. Courtesy Herald-Examiner Collection, Los Angeles Public Library.

participation on future projects.[59] By the time work began on the first Bullock's Fashion Square shopping center in Santa Ana in 1956, Shellhorn's word was enough to authorize substantial changes to an initial architectural site plan by Pereira & Luckman.[60] This collaborative relationship continued after Mahlon E. Arnett succeeded Winnett as president in 1964. Shellhorn attributed the success of the Bullock's projects to the strength of their shared vision (fig. 18).

The Bullock's Pasadena commission brought with it new responsibilities and the potential for more high-profile projects. This increased workload led Shellhorn to form a business partnership with her husband (fig. 19). Kueser, who lacked a college education, had assumed some financial tasks and handled client correspondence after his retirement at the end of 1944. Over the next year, however, he took courses in drafting, learned to prepare construction drawings, and worked with her in the field surveying smaller properties. He also became fluent in Spanish, a vital bridge in working with crews, and took a six-month construction job to gain the experience necessary to fully supervise the installation of Shellhorn's designs.

Kueser's assistance liberated his wife from managerial tasks, leaving her free to dedicate herself to the creative aspects of her work and tackle a greater range of increasingly complex, high-profile projects. This business model was unusual not only because of their untraditional gender roles, but also because of the firm's ability to acquire major commissions. At a time when larger landscape architecture firms were taking on the bigger commercial projects, independent designers tended to focus on residential work or form associations with other firms. Shellhorn's business continued to succeed because it brought the best of a small practice—personal attention to each project, absolute control over design, meticulous supervision of installation, and long-term maintenance—to the kind of projects that would otherwise have gone to larger firms.

Bullock's Pasadena was also Shellhorn's first collaboration with Welton Becket, Winnett's architect. It was a part-

Figure 19. Shellhorn and Harry Kueser in their studio office, 1955. Courtesy RSP.

nership that would prove mutually beneficial for both professionals and play a significant role in the success of her independent practice. Becket had come to Los Angeles and begun his architectural partnership, Wurdeman & Becket, with Walter Wurdeman in 1933, the same year Shellhorn returned from Cornell University to begin her own practice. Becket was a few years older and already well known when he and Shellhorn met in 1945, but they immediately recognized each other as kindred spirits. Both were highly principled and placed great importance on personal integrity. Both were from the generation of designers whose careers would parallel the rise of California modernism, and the success of their collaboration derived from a mutual respect for each other's abilities and a shared design sensibility.[61]

Early in the 1930s Wurdeman & Becket had embraced a philosophy of "total design," persuading clients to let the firm manage master planning, engineering, interior work, and landscape design. Shellhorn appreciated the functional and aesthetic consistency of this approach. The opportunity to create a landscape plan in tandem with the building design allowed her not only to witness the building process but also to have a say in the final project. Shellhorn's belief that the client came first was echoed in Becket's view that "a building should reflect the client, not the architect."[62] Bullock's Pasadena launched Becket's firm into commercial architecture, and it gave Shellhorn the kind of recognition that resulted in new public commissions as well as inquiries from wealthy residential clients.

With Bullock's Pasadena, Shellhorn learned the value of collaborating with architects and participating in the early stages of a project. Her view of the landscape architect's role included grading, drainage, irrigation systems, paving construction, lighting, soil preparation, planting design, and erosion control, all of which would have an impact on the final design. Although Shellhorn believed that architects could manage these design elements on some projects, she later wrote about the importance of having landscape architects involved from an early stage. With this type of collaboration, she noted, "problems are better solved, plant areas are adequate and in the right places to achieve the desired effects, irrigation systems are worked out to best take care of the various types of materials and exposures, lighting is directly related to the landscape plan, and the whole problem is studied by the architect and the landscape architect to attain the best use, organization, and design of the areas involved."[63] Shellhorn was proud of her technical knowledge as well as her design skills, and collaborative projects gave her the opportunity to share it.

By the close of 1947, Shellhorn had finished her landscape design for Bullock's Palm Springs. Welton Becket's firm also separately engaged Shellhorn for the Prudential Insurance Western Home Office in Los Angeles (fig. 20), one of the city's major postwar structures, and recommended Shellhorn to create landscape plans for a residence for the wealthy oilman Henry Salvatori and his wife in Bel-Air. She also continued her association with Frank Green, working on the Cal Bing housing development in Van Nuys, and completing about a dozen residential landscape designs, many of them including installation and maintenance contracts.

As she neared the end of her tenure as ASLA chapter president, Shellhorn increasingly put planning at the forefront of her meeting agenda. In November 1947 she led a group of members on a weekend tour of major planning projects in San Diego's Mission Bay area: the Linda Vista housing project and shopping center, Presidio Park, and the Cabrillo freeway. She was fascinated with the combined scope of these proj-

Figure 20. Prudential Square, northeast view across Wilshire Boulevard, 1949. Photograph by Douglas M. Simmonds. In the author's possession.

ects, which she called "a stupendous undertaking for a city the size of San Diego."[64] She also steered the chapter toward supporting city planning efforts and the implementation of zoning ordinances. By 1948 she was devoting more than half of the year's schedule to planning issues in the Coachella Valley, Pasadena, Long Beach, Glendale, and Santa Barbara.[65] Her approach to site design reflected a growing awareness of the environment, concern for its conservation, and the need to acknowledge and manage human use—values later articulated in such classic books as Kevin Lynch's *Site Planning* (1962), Lawrence Halprin's *R.S.V.P. Cycles* (1969), and Ian McHarg's *Design with Nature* (1969).

While Shellhorn became an advocate for the profession during this early postwar period, she did not always agree with her colleagues about the philosophical basis of land-scape design. Garrett Eckbo, a modernist who differentiated his approach as landscape *design*, experimented with radical forms to express the new "social landscaping" of midcentury landscape architecture, and published his ideas in *Landscape for Living* (1950).[66] Although Shellhorn did not dismiss modernist ideals, she disapproved of experimental landscape designs and modernist exercises devoid of site or client. For her, a primary purpose of landscape architecture was to instill a sense of physical well-being. She later wrote: "We are presently living in an age of great upheavals, change and vitality, an age which is exhausting with its tensions, noise, frustrations, rush, and distractions. Much landscape architecture which is created today reflects this atmosphere. It is full of ideas, too full, distracting in its many opposing lines, gimmicks, accents, spot planting, angular patterns, countless different elements, and garish colors. Many of the designs are clever, and good from a design standpoint, but exhausting. To meet a clever, witty, sparkling individual is a stimulating experience, but to be with that person constantly, leaves no peace."[67]

By the late 1940s Shellhorn's work was gaining notice from both her professional peers and the public. She began an association with the architect Wallace Neff in September 1948, eventually completing residential landscape designs with him for Dr. and Mrs. L. John Tragerman in Los Angeles (1948); Edgar and Flossie Richards in Cheviot Hills (1949–1952) and Palm Springs (1955); and John and Rella Factor in Beverly Hills (1953; fig. 21). She also designed another commercial landscape for Becket, Rheem Manufacturing in Southgate (1948), which was soon followed by a demonstration home for the Kaiser-Burns development in Panorama City (1949).

Figure 21. Factor garden, 1953. Photograph by Ruth Shellhorn. Courtesy RSP.

As her network expanded, other wealthy clients turned to Shellhorn. R. Stanton Avery, inventor of the self-adhesive label and founder and CEO of the corporation now known as Avery Dennison, commissioned her for residential landscape designs in South Pasadena (1951), Bradbury (1954), and Pasadena (1976). Edward W. Carter, a retail business magnate and University of California regent, hired her to design gardens for his homes in Los Angeles (1956) and Bel-Air (1965 and 1975). Her work also caught the attention of a small group of Hollywood actors, which led to a series of commissions: garden designs at Gene Autry's residence in North Hollywood (1950; fig. 22) and his business office in Hollywood (1952), as well as landscape designs for Spencer Tracy and his wife at the John Tracy Clinic in Los Angeles (1951) and their residence in Encino (1953), and a residential garden for Barbara Stanwyck in Westwood (1951).

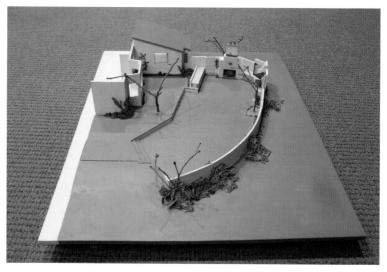

Figure 22. Model of Autry garden built by Shellhorn and Kueser, 1950.
Courtesy RSP.

During this time, Bullock's continued to offer Shellhorn work, seeking her services on a major landscape redesign for Bullock's Wilshire in Los Angeles (designed in 1929 by the father-and-son architectural firm Parkinson & Parkinson) in 1952. In this case, because virtually all of the architectural elements were already in place, Shellhorn's contribution was a detailed planting plan. She designed each area as a composition, much as a set designer might, and spared no effort to locate exactly the right plant for each situation; a tree scout was enlisted to find specimens, like the shapely ornamental pear that arched over a walkway at a back entrance.[68] She knew the value of prime specimens. When a new parking structure was built at the Pasadena store in 1956, Shellhorn boxed the whole set of matching magnolia trees and saved them to use in the new Bullock's Fashion Square shopping center in Santa Ana.[69]

Shellhorn's collaboration with Becket also continued, as the architect came to trust her unreservedly, presenting her with increasingly more complex and high-profile projects. In 1952 he turned to her at the last minute to help him rescue a landscape plan for the Stonestown shopping center in San Francisco. After considering how to achieve the best effects for the buildings, she rearranged the already purchased plants on the sixty-five-acre site and gave suggestions for additional plant material and placement. Becket was gratified with the results; her intervention was a compromise, but it enhanced the quality of his project.[70] Their work together also included a Prudential Insurance building in Menlo Park in the San Francisco Bay area (1954), a design that Shellhorn prepared for Becket as a favor, and designs for his addition to the Veteran's Administration Hospital in Long Beach (1955) and the Santa Monica Civic Auditorium (1956; fig. 23). In 1957 she drafted a new landscape plan for a branch

Figure 23. Santa Monica Civic Auditorium, 1958. Photograph by Julius Shulman. Courtesy © J. Paul Getty Trust. Getty Research Institute, Los Angeles (2004.R.10).

of the Buffums' department store chain in Santa Ana, which Becket had designed seven years before.

In early 1955, Becket recommended Shellhorn to his friend Walt Disney, who was struggling to unify the different sections of his new theme park in Anaheim. In the few months before Disneyland's opening, Shellhorn designed a pedestrian plan and details for the park's entrance, Town Square (fig. 24), and Main Street. To unify the overall plan, she created a planting scheme for the central Plaza Hub garden that related to the entrances of each area of the park. As a consultant for Disney, she worked with an all-male group of designers responsible for the entire enterprise, contributing to many facets of the project, including grading and other engineering details. One of the most innovative aspects of

Disneyland—its ability to transport the visitor to distant lands of fantasy and adventure—can be partly attributed to Shellhorn's use of colorful, vibrant plants, skillfully selected and expertly organized.

Up to the mid-1950s, Shellhorn had relied on the backing of male architects, landscape architects, and businessmen as her primary source of commissions. The wives of these men were also some of the Southland's most important figures and would soon become equally enthusiastic promoters of her work. In 1955, Dorothy Buffum Chandler, the Buffums' department stores heiress and the driving force behind development of the Los Angeles Music Center, played an instrumental part in securing work and recognition for Shellhorn. In her role as an editor for the *Los Angeles Times* (her husband was the newspaper's pub-

Figure 24. Town Square, Disneyland, 1955. In the author's possession.

lisher, Norman Chandler), she nominated Shellhorn for a Los Angeles Times Woman of the Year award after learning of her work at Disneyland and Bullock's Wilshire. The ensuing publicity led to a cascade of commissions for Shellhorn, many of them initiated by members of a group of wealthy women that included leaders of charitable organizations, benefactors of the arts, writers, actors, and members of the financial community. They referred her to their friends, their family members, and their husband's businesses; Shellhorn's correspondence files reveal that they took delight in the association, one calling Shellhorn "a very superior lady," and another declaring, "[We] feel that we are lucky to have you in the driver's seat."[71]

In 1956 Shellhorn created an original adaptation of a Mediterranean garden for the Chandlers' home in the Hancock Park neighborhood of Los Angeles. Soon after, while serving on the University of California Board of Regents, Chandler secured Shellhorn's appointment as consulting landscape architect for the rapidly expanding University of California campus in Riverside. Chandler persuaded the board to bypass such better-known contenders as Ralph Cornell and Tommy Tomson. Much later Shellhorn recalled the coup with gratitude and amusement, commenting that "she thought it was about time they had a woman landscape architect."[72]

If she never publicly acknowledged the challenge of being a female landscape architect in her public writings or interviews, Shellhorn described her experience in her diaries, admitting the difficulty of attracting high-profile commissions in the earlier years, but also acknowledging that her gender was an asset in getting the commission for the UC Riverside campus. The positive public face she presented to the world is expressed in a 1955 response to a student's letter asking about prospects for female landscape architects. She wrote: "As to a woman in the field. This does not enter into it at all. I have never thought of myself as a woman in competition with men, but rather as a Landscape Architect trying to do the best job I can, and I have never come across prejudice because I am a woman. In fact I have had clients who preferred a woman, feeling that they are more sensitive than men especially in garden design."[73]

The UC Riverside project gave Shellhorn her first opportunity to reflect more deeply on her aesthetic philosophy and approach to design. In 1961, while working on the campus plan, she wrote "Thoughts on Landscape Architecture," an unpublished essay that would become her personal manifesto. In it, she described the importance of designing in response to the site, having empathy for the client, and rejecting orthodoxy, among other topics. Shellhorn begins by broadly defining the parameters of landscape architecture and mandating on-site evaluation as the only means of successfully considering the context of a plan, noting that "a particular garden or other site should be developed in itself, but also as a part of a larger picture to be successful, for the picture takes in all that the eye encompasses," and that "distant views of mountains, valleys, the sea, a composition of trees outside the property, or a particular feature in the distance may be brought into the picture."[74] She builds on this theme to explain the philosophy behind her larger commercial and campus projects, especially her concurrent work on the UC Riverside master landscape plan. In order to discover "the 'personality' of the site," she recommends responding to existing landforms rather than imposing any standard methodology of design, writing that a "designer should spend much time on the site just getting the feeling of it: the topography, exposures, views, existing trees, and other physical characteristics." She criticizes the practice of "whipping the site into submission" as "an attempt of the ego for supremacy." In contrast, she advocates for "a little more humility and a reverence for natural beauty." Her determination to preserve the arroyos on the Riverside campus is a particularly powerful example of her concern for the environment (fig. 25).

Shellhorn cared not only about how people used the spaces she designed, but also how they felt about her landscapes. She advised her fellow designers to "mentally project [themselves] into the lives of the clients for a while to try to feel as they do about their problems and their wishes

Figure 25. University of California, Riverside, Administration building, north patio, 1976. Photograph by Ruth Shellhorn. Courtesy RSP.

for the use of the area to be designed," adding, "There is a need here for understanding, sensitivity, and a desire to serve, rather than an opportunity for the designer to express his own ideas exclusively." On behalf of her clients, Shellhorn viewed her role as a provider of natural respite, and she considered this to be a central purpose of her work. She saw herself creating "places of peace, rest, relaxation, and inspiration, places where the soul may expand as the mind becomes quiet, where there is possibility for spiritual renewal." Her work was, in part, a response to both the rapid urbanization of the era and the egoism characterizing much of modern design—"too many architectural features clamoring for attention, and the sparkling cleverness of over designed areas."

In "Thoughts on Landscape Architecture," Shellhorn also stressed the need for landscape architects to envision their designs in three dimensions, an exercise she emphasized throughout her career. When her husband joined the practice he built models to her specifications, and these soon became a regular part of her design process. The models allowed her to see the individual elements of a plan as part of a larger entity and to coordinate spaces in which multiple architects or architectural firms contributed structures. At Bullock's Fashion Square La Habra, for example, Welton Becket served as project architect and designed the Bullock's store; Killingsworth, Brady & Associates designed the Buffums' department store; and Skidmore, Owings & Merrill designed Joseph Magnin's. As Shellhorn explained, "The development of one building site must be seen in the mind with its proper backgrounds blending into the rest of the area harmoniously. This same approach was used in the Fashion Squares, where divergent building styles, such as at La Habra, were given their own setting, yet by means of subtle transitions and certain repetition of elements on into the site, a flowing harmonious composition was achieved for the whole site."

After eight years of work at UC Riverside, Shellhorn had completed a landscape master plan and dozens of specific designs for various areas of the campus. She developed excellent working relationships with several of the project architects, including members of the firm of Killingsworth, Brady, which designed the cafeteria, student center, and bookstore in 1963. Although she found the position satisfying, she realized that the increasing workload would necessitate either hiring employees or giving up a substantial number of other projects, including a redesign of Buffums' in Santa Ana. She reluctantly stepped down in 1964. Campus planning continued to interest her, however, and she later accepted consulting landscape positions at El Camino College in Torrance (1970–1978) and Scripps College in Claremont (1981). She also created landscape designs for private secondary schools, including the Marlborough School in Los Angeles (1967–1993), the Harvard School (now the Harvard-Westlake School) in North Hollywood (1974–1990), and the Chadwick School on the Palos Verdes Peninsula (1982). Campus planning gave Shellhorn the opportunity to take control over the full scope of a project, as well as the details, just as Florence Yoch had advised. When Shellhorn began her career this was not a commonplace practice, but she and her colleagues staked their claim in the postwar era, and she was thus able to declare, "In our campus planning, everything outside the building is the landscape architect's province."

Now free from her obligations at UC Riverside, Shellhorn joined up with Becket again to collaborate on a Bullock's Fashion Square shopping center in Sherman Oaks (1962); the Mutual Savings and Loan Association in Pasadena (1964), where she designed a plaza and plantings that continue to inspire landscape architects; a Bullock's department store at Lakewood Center (1965); and the Fashion Square Del Amo shopping center in Torrance (1966) and Fashion Square La Habra (1968). With their colorful gardens, inviting seating areas, fountains, shade trees, and abundant parking, the shopping centers further encouraged the concept of shopping as a pleasant outdoor activity (figs. 26 and 27). Bullock's Fashion Square La Habra, completed the year before Becket's death in 1969, marked their final collaboration.

Figure 26. Shellhorn overseeing the planting of palm trees, Bullock's Fashion Square Del Amo, 1966. Photograph by Harry Kueser. In the author's possession.

Figure 27. Parking bays at Fashion Square La Habra, 1972. Photograph by Dominick Culotta. In the author's possession.

Shellhorn's devotion to her clients is perhaps best exemplified through her work for Charles and Nancy Munger from 1966 to 1988. Nancy Munger was an alumna and trustee of the Marlborough School in Los Angeles. Shellhorn completed the landscape plan for the school in 1967, and a year later the Mungers commissioned her to design their own garden in Hancock Park. In 1974, Charles was instrumental in having Shellhorn hired to create landscape plans for the Harvard School in North Hollywood, where he served as a trustee. The Mungers also recommended Shellhorn to design residential plans for their two adult daughters, both in Pasadena (1983 and 1988). Like many of her clients, the Mungers appreciated Shellhorn's design aesthetic, her ability to deliver a project on time and on budget, and her exacting expectation of quality from the designers, engineers, and contractors with whom she worked. She developed a formidable reputation for enforcing her unwavering standards on the construction site. One former worker recalled, "If she specified plants to be spaced six inches apart, she expected the contractor to use a six-inch ruler to make sure he got it right. If he didn't get it right, she got down on her knees, in a skirt, and showed him how to do the work."[75] As Charles Munger remarked, "Ruth was a quiet fanatic about quality work." Munger, a financial partner with Warren Buffett for Berkshire Hathaway, who could afford any landscape architect, chose Shellhorn to create the designs for his estate and the educational institutions he and Nancy supported.[76]

In October 1967, *Landscape Design and Construction* devoted a substantial part of the issue to Shellhorn's Bullock's projects. This was the only publication that discussed her landscape architectural career in a manner aimed at professionals who wished to understand her work. The department stores were also featured in a March 1969 *Sunset Magazine* article, "Shopping for Landscape Ideas," which illustrated how elements from all four of the Bullock's Fashion Squares could be used in the home garden.[77] Homeowners had been writing letters directly to Shellhorn for years, asking her to identify particular plants and seeking advice on how to give their own gardens that coveted, sun-drenched aura. The article addressed some of those questions, as well as many of the inquiries from homeowners to *Sunset*'s garden design editor.

Although they focused on only one aspect of a lifetime of professional achievement and hard work, the two publications secured Shellhorn's prominence as a gifted and thoughtful practitioner. This was fortunate because, in spite of her creative confidence, Shellhorn did not seek publicity. Reserved and modest, she was brought up to believe that publication might make her appear to be seeking work in a manner she considered undignified.[78] As early as 1949, Shellhorn had written of her desire "for some recognition from the architects so that we'd get more work from them," but called herself "too chicken to do any selling like Eckbo, etc."[79] David Streatfield has noted the "terrible imbalance in terms of the public's perception between Ruth Shellhorn . . . and many of her contemporaries, such as Garrett Eckbo, Lawrence Halprin, and Thomas Church, who wrote books about their own work, hired professional photographers, and published extensively."[80] Perhaps this is where gender most undermined Shellhorn's achieving a place in histories of landscape architecture.

In 1971, Shellhorn's old friend and colleague George Huntington successfully nominated her as a Fellow of the American Society of Landscape Architects. Her fellowship was granted for "excellence in executed work." At the time of her induction, Shellhorn was the only woman Fellow on the West Coast, and one of only ten in the country. Not more than eight ASLA fellowships were awarded each year by the organization, then numbering some 3,000 members, and there were only 145 fellows nationwide.[81] Unlike self-promotion, the notice of her peers was something she valued highly.

Throughout the next two decades, Shellhorn would juggle planning and long-term maintenance contracts with the commercial and residential projects of a small, busy firm. In 1973 she accepted a position as consulting landscape architect for the community association in Rolling Hills, a gated community on the Palos Verde Peninsula first developed in the 1930s. Twice a month for the next nineteen years, she met with board members to refine and oversee application of the association's CCRs (codes, covenants, and restrictions) to a multiacre common area of roads, right-of-ways, and open space. She also reviewed residential design proposals for development. Her work as a supervisor of long-term maintenance for Bullock's continued until the late 1970s, when her husband's declining health forced him to retire from their practice. Although Shellhorn focused on residential work after Kueser's retirement, she continued campus planning and created a landscape design for Bay Island Park in Newport Beach in 1987.[82]

Shellhorn's domestic commissions of the 1970s and 1980s represent an exceptionally creative period of her career. At midcentury, her early residential work had informed her commercial and other nonresidential landscape designs; as a more mature designer, she now brought the perception, skill, and experience of her public projects back to her private gardens. These included a hillside garden overlooking the Pacific Ocean for Pat and George Johnson in Rolling Hills, with the architect Edward Killingsworth (1970–1972; fig. 28); a small garden for Mr. and Mrs. Henry Mudd in Westwood for a home designed by Roland Coate in 1968 (1972); a reconception of a landscape design created by the Galper-Baldon firm for Mr. and Mrs. Charles

Figure 28. Johnson garden, 2012. Photograph by author.

Ducommun in Bel-Air (1974–1981); a modernization of an English-style estate garden in Pasadena for Ernestine and R. Stanton Avery (1976–1984); a sculpture garden for Adelaide and Alexander Hixon in Pasadena, with the architect A. Quincy Jones (1975–1978; fig. 29); and a garden for Antonia Brackenridge Niven near the arroyo in San Marino for a home originally designed by Garrett Van Pelt (1980–1987).

When she was in her early seventies, Shellhorn altered gardens designed by Garrett Eckbo for the architect Carl Maston in Los Angeles (1982–1985), and for one of Maston's clients, Samuel Hellinger, in Pacific Palisades (1982–1986). Eckbo represented the cutting edge in modernist residential landscape design, but in these two cases, Shellhorn and her clients believed his paper presentations offered more promise than the realized products.[83] Shellhorn's experience in remodeling gardens had begun in the early 1950s, when she

Figure 29. Hixon garden, 1978. Photograph by Ruth Shellhorn. Courtesy RSP.

updated landscapes designed by Florence Yoch for Scribner Birlenbach in West Los Angeles and Mr. and Mrs. Lawrence Brooks in Pasadena. Working with Yoch's former clients, she went to great pains to preserve design elements of gardens cherished by their owners. Considering Yoch's role in inspiring Shellhorn to pursue her profession, it is fitting that Shellhorn's final project was a meticulous restoration of one of Yoch's finest surviving Pasadena gardens. From 1978 until the early 1990s, she incrementally restored the garden for the novelist Harriet Doerr (fig. 30). A few years after Shellhorn completed her work, Doerr wrote an article for *Architectural Digest,* expressing the profound meaning she found in this

Figure 30. Doerr garden, 1987. Photograph by Robert M. Fletcher. Courtesy Burton and Patricia Fletcher.

landscape throughout her life, a garden she described as having "invaded all of my remembered past."[84] Shellhorn retired after preserving this historic landscape.

Although Shellhorn remains a little-known figure in the history of the profession, her contribution to the region was acknowledged during her lifetime, particularly through her collaboration with Welton Becket. The work of Shellhorn and Becket not only helped shape a regional aesthetic but also elevated the profile of Los Angeles. In 2003, when the Los Angeles Conservancy celebrated Becket's lifetime achievement, Shellhorn was the only landscape architect, and the only woman, invited to participate on the panel discussion of his work. Louis Naidorf, Becket's lead architect for the Capitol Records building in Hollywood, affirmed their collaboration, asserting that "with architect Welton Becket, Shellhorn put postwar Los Angeles on the map."

The lasting impact of Shellhorn's and Becket's collaborative effort is still observable throughout the city.[85]

•

In September 2004, twenty-five years after first meeting Ruth Shellhorn, I called her on a whim, knowing that if she was alive she would be in her mid-nineties. She answered the phone, and I discovered that she still led an active life. Our conversation led to an invitation to visit her studio. She showed me floor-to-ceiling cabinets containing all of her original drawings on tissue and vellum, neatly labeled, alphabetically organized, and covered with the plastic bags from which she removed her copy of the *Los Angeles Times* each morning. These drawings included her original plans for Disneyland, the Bullock's projects, the landscape development plans for the University of California at Riverside, and hundreds of other drawings that collectively represented the scope of midcentury landscape architectural design in the Los Angeles region. She also showed me her client files, each containing detailed plant lists, correspondence, time sheets, construction schedules, and hand-drawn sketches, all filed and boxed by decade. I later learned that she kept copies of the articles she had written, articles by others featuring her work, and photographs of her landscapes published in books, trade magazines, and popular publications. After the introduction of Kodachrome slide film in 1936, she began to take before-and-after color slides of her projects. These, too, were carefully labeled and filed. Throughout her career, she kept an alphabetically organized card file of her clients and a handwritten note above her drafting table, *"ALWAYS DOUBLE CHECK."*[86]

Realizing that Shellhorn's collection was an invaluable asset to the study of midcentury landscape architecture, I urged her to donate her papers to a suitable institution. She agreed, allowing me to make inquiries to several, and ultimately selected the Charles E. Young Research Library at UCLA. These records preserve detailed information about Shellhorn's design process and philosophy, reflecting her perception of a project's place in time, the geographical context of its site, the client's purpose, and the quality of response from those who owned and visited her gardens. While her photographs constitute an invaluable visual record of her constructed projects, they also offer a rare glimpse into how she intended her gardens to be experienced. As we began the task of reviewing her plans and files, it became clear that much of her work no longer existed. Over the next two years I interviewed Shellhorn every three weeks, taking detailed notes about her life and work.

In 2005, a review of Cornell University records revealed that Shellhorn had actually earned the requisite units for two bachelor degrees, one in landscape architecture and a second in architecture.[87] Both degrees were finally awarded in June 2005, the year she received an ASLA Lifetime Achievement Award. Although this belated recognition underscored her accomplishments—particularly that of launching her own practice in the Depression without the support of academic credentials—this book is the first major effort to include her work in the history of landscape architecture. Shellhorn was still living in her Redondo Beach home until a few days before she died, on November 3, 2006, at age ninety-seven.

During her long and productive career, Shellhorn continually impressed fellow practitioners with the breadth of her knowledge in all aspects of the field. She was an expert in regional plants with a strong background in architecture and

Shellhorn outside her home in Redondo Beach, 2005. Photograph by Ken Hively. Los Angeles Times photo, © 2005. Reprinted with permission.

engineering. She had an intuitive understanding of the California landscape, as well as a keen ability to capture its essence in modern design. She understood that the rising tide of consumerism fueled by California's increasing prosperity required new forms for contemporary living, and yet she cherished the past. As a planner, she designed for the automobile in a manner that preserved a shoreline threatened by development. In her designs for department stores, she found ways to slow down the pace of life, both to encourage shopping and to provide a respite from it. Her campus plans fostered a sense of community, while inviting teachers and students to acknowledge the natural rhythms of their larger environment. In residential gardens, she created havens for the imagination that somehow fit perfectly into the native landscape. At Disneyland, she used plants as a means of creating imaginary worlds both fantastic and familiar.

Shellhorn's landscapes stretched the boundaries of modernism within a traditional context, always anticipating change over time, as plantings matured. In the course of a career lasting nearly sixty years, she helped shape Southern California's iconic twentieth-century design aesthetic. A master of modern landscape design, Ruth Shellhorn should be remembered not only for this achievement, but for her personal and professional dedication to enhancing and protecting the landscape.

SOUTH PASADENA
HIGH SCHOOL

SOUTH PASADENA, CALIFORNIA

1935–1938

In June 1935 Shellhorn received her first public commission—a series of landscape designs for South Pasadena High School, where she had graduated with the class of 1927. The project came to her through a recommendation from her high school art teacher and was funded by the Works Progress Administration. Over a three-year period, Shellhorn created designs for the Art Court, the courtyards in front of the Fine Arts and Science buildings (1936), and the girls' athletic field (1937).

The original building, designed by local architects Norman Foote Marsh and Clarence H. Russell, opened in 1907 in a South Pasadena neighborhood north of downtown Los Angeles.[1] By 1935 the school had grown significantly and, despite the Depression, two new modernist-style buildings were commissioned.[2] Mirror images, the buildings faced each other across separate courtyards of lawn intersected by walkways. A small pool was tucked into the Science building courtyard and an existing Catalina Island cherry tree incorporated into the Fine Arts courtyard.

In 1935 Shellhorn was a young landscape architect searching for her own identifiable style. She struggled with the planting design, trying to decide between a traditional palette of deciduous and flowering trees and shrubs or a more modern approach. After much consideration, she resolved the issue in her sleep: "On waking, the solution to my problem was there clear as life all solved. Something told me to use palms as I had formerly considered and the way it came

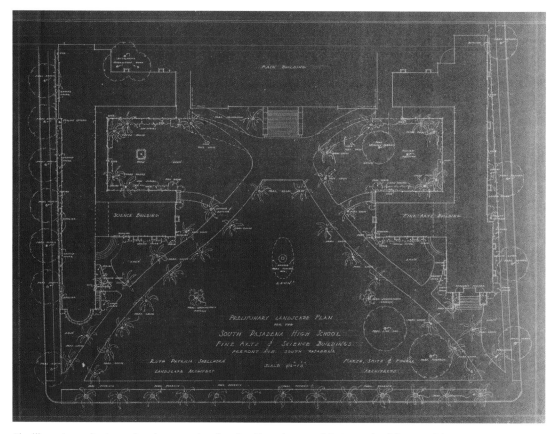

Shellhorn's preliminary landscape plan for the Fine Arts and Science buildings, 1935. Courtesy RSP.

Pencil sketch of the Fine Arts building, 1936. In the author's possession.

out was so clean cut and with no alternatives—funny, as if it had been given to me."[3] The planting scheme she settled on shows the beginnings of her experiments with evergreens and suggests the regional aesthetic she would develop later in her career.

Palm trees had provided a signature element in the high school's landscape since at least the 1920s, when Shellhorn matriculated. She continued this tradition by using palms to provide continuity throughout the campus. She worked with two Washington fan palms that stood as sentinels at the school entrance; defined pathways with single cocos palms, which she also clustered at various building corners; continued the existing line of phoenix palms used as street trees; and specified smaller palm trees, such as seaforthia, for planting beds. This liberal use of palms created a kind of overall ceiling throughout the rambling campus and defined it as a

Science building courtyard, 1936. Photograph by Ruth Shellhorn. In the author's possession.

distinct place. The understory for this canopy featured large-leaved philodendron and thick clusters of giant bird-of-paradise. Tam junipers, in planters on either side of the entrance to the Fine Arts building, and native arbutus shrubs, a reference to the native oak trees throughout the adjacent neighborhood, gave the composition a rich pattern without the monotony typical of many subtropical landscapes.

Shellhorn's landscape design for the Art Court was more detailed and structured, a departure from her free-form planting scheme throughout the campus. She took particular care with this area, creating a brick-walled enclave around an existing carob tree that became a "secret garden" for students seeking a quiet space. She designed a brick seat around the tree, used brick patio pavers on sand with grass joints to tie the horizontal plane into an adjacent lawn, and included sentimental elements in the garden, such as a brick bench donated to the high school by the class of 1927 and a bas-relief ceramic tile embedded in the brick wall.

The project's relatively intensive labor requirements were driven primarily by the abundant supply of cheap labor flooding the Southland during the mid-1930s. The WPA provided funding for the sought-after construction jobs, and Shellhorn found herself supervising untrained workers, including lawyers and other professionals from all walks of life.[4] Their lack of skill and experience infuriated her, and she confided to her diary, "Never again!"[5]

Shellhorn's own inexperience in this early work is illustrated by her lack of attention to maintenance considerations. Although she specified local plants with increasing

Art Court, 1936. Photograph by Ruth Shellhorn. In the author's possession.

assurance, she quickly realized that her initial planting plan included small potted plants and delicate flowering annuals requiring an unrealistic level of care. With some guidance from Ralph Cornell, she addressed these problems in a written review she conducted for the school district in 1938.[6] From that point forward, Shellhorn considered plans for the long-term maintenance of her landscapes a hallmark of her practice.

Over time, the Art Court at South Pasadena High School developed a special allure, becoming a place of refuge, the site of outdoor classes, and a focal point of the campus, where parents took photographs of their graduating seniors. Even after part of the court was destroyed to make room for a library, the garden continued to inspire affection and nostalgia from students and faculty.[7] Seventy years after completing this design, Shellhorn received a letter from a former student, now elderly and living in Germany, who wanted to thank her for creating such a memorable space.[8]

SHORELINE DEVELOPMENT STUDY

LOS ANGELES COUNTY, CALIFORNIA

1943–1944

In March 1943, at a time when commissions were scarce, Shellhorn had a stroke of good fortune that would significantly influence the course of her developing practice. Her neighbor Joseph Mellen, assistant county regional planner, recommended her for a full-time planning position with the Greater Los Angeles Citizens Committee. Eager to find steady work, Shellhorn wrote a letter of inquiry expressing her "hope that [her] . . . genuine appreciation of planning in all of its phases, and enthusiasm for problems and hard work may be considered." She went on to say that as "a native daughter of Los Angeles" she "wanted to have a finger in her future development," and that she found "a broadness of scope and a much greater opportunity for creative expression, in regional planning than . . . other work."[1] She got the job.

Although the absence of men during wartime was a factor in Shellhorn's obtaining the position, the trend toward

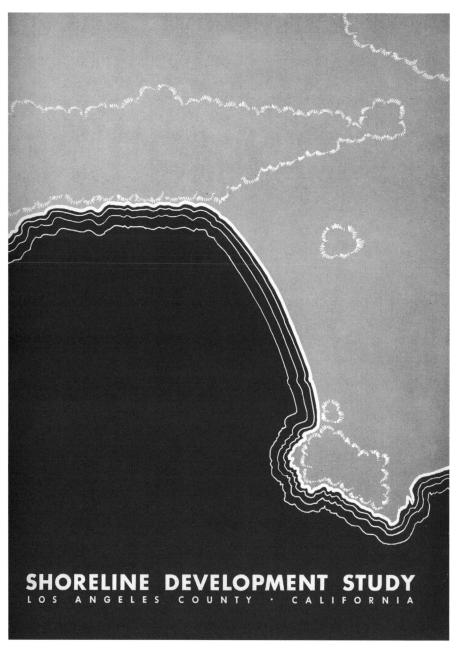

Shoreline Development Study, cover, 1944. In the author's possession.

requiring specialized training for participation in larger projects also favored her. She joined the all-male office as an equal. The committee was created to work cooperatively with regional city and county agencies. Led by P. G. Winnett, president of the Bullock's department stores, and the architect Carl McElvy, it was funded by a private group of civic-minded businessmen whose mission was to develop current and postwar plans for regional recreation and transportation infrastructure.[2] For Shellhorn, this new opportunity would provide the professional connections and experience necessary to become an influential landscape architect.

The purpose of the Shoreline Development Study was to analyze and make recommendations for improving a neglected eleven-mile stretch of coast between Playa del Rey and Palos Verdes. The report provided graphic examples of pollution from local industries, as well as the lack of an infrastructure to support tourism. To begin resolving these problems, the committee's report recommended a development plan that addressed the need for a highway system with a shoreline parkway and multiple beach parking areas. It also advocated continuity in beach development, so that swimming beaches, fishing areas, pleasure piers, and regional parks were evenly distributed along the entire span of coastline and all beaches included parking, restrooms, dressing rooms, food concessions, and lifeguard stations.[3] The plan provided landscape designs for regional parks in the cities of El Segundo, Manhattan Beach, Torrance, and Redondo Beach / Hermosa Beach. The plan for El Segundo proposed relocating a sewage screening plant to create unobstructed views of its two hundred acres of dunes; in Manhattan Beach, a new park made use of a naturally sheltered site and focused on areas for sports and an outdoor theater; the Torrance park featured bridle trails, a trailer camp, pic-

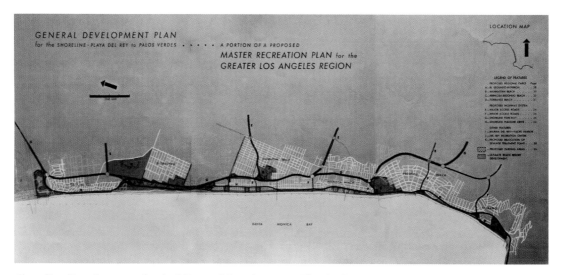

Shoreline Development Study, "General Development Plan," 1944. In the author's possession.

nic groves, and walking paths situated on sixty-five acres of bluff overlooking the ocean; and the Redondo / Hermosa park plan suggested repurposing an abandoned electric railway as a link to the shoreline pleasure drive, clearing a salt marsh for boating, and transforming an old steam plant into a community center.[4]

This was Shellhorn's first opportunity to work collaboratively with a group of design professionals. She contributed to the layout and graphics of the final report, including her own designs for the four oceanfront regional parks, as well as the research and statistical analysis informing them. She also created highway access and parking plans for each park. Even at this stage of her career, Shellhorn was promoting the liberal use of trees and landscape design in parking areas, a practice she would build on in her Bullock's department store projects. She wrote the accompanying text for each of the park designs, explaining how recreational demand

and site conditions were considered in developing each park program.

Today environmental analysis reports are a staple of modern planning, but in 1944 the requirements of these new

Plan for Manhattan Beach Regional Park, 1944. Courtesy RSP.

studies were unclear. As a precursor of contemporary environmental planning documents, the Shoreline Development Study is particularly noteworthy for its prescient recommendations for political and social action. A harbinger of later restrictions on oil drilling in Santa Monica Bay, the study articulated many of the protection goals that would eventually become part of the California Environmental Quality Act (1970) and the California Coastal Act (1972), advocated for the use of public funding for recreation and parkland acquisition, and paved the way for installation of the first sewage treatment plant in Los Angeles and the development of Marina del Rey.

Shellhorn's park designs gave the Shoreline Development Study the rich level of detail that led to its publication in 1944.[5] Although the parks in the plan were never developed because of the demand for postwar housing on the sites, the project became a cornerstone document for Los Angeles County's revision of its 1940 Master Plan of Shoreline Development.[6] Shellhorn's work on the committee earned her the recognition and appreciation of McElvy and Winnett and led to her first commission for a major commercial landscape, Bullock's Pasadena.

BULLOCK'S PASADENA

PASADENA, CALIFORNIA

1945–1980; OPENED 1947

As early as 1937, Bullock's president P. G. Winnett anticipated an economic boom and began planning for the first suburban Bullock's department store in Pasadena. In 1945 he turned to his Shoreline Development Study colleague Carl McElvy for advice on the selection of an architect for the new store. McElvy recommended hiring Welton Becket of Wurdeman & Becket, and Becket returned the favor by subcontracting the site planning and landscape design to McElvy, who immediately brought Shellhorn on board as his junior associate. When McElvy was offered the position of campus architect at UCLA just a few months later, he turned the commission over to Shellhorn with Winnett's approval. By the end of 1946, Shellhorn controlled the project as the lead landscape architect. Recognizing the enormous opportunity, she "worked to make it right, and never looked back."[1]

Becket planned the three-level department store to hug

a gently sloping site of more than eight acres, designing the building to emphasize open space, horizontality, and convenience. He employed a "moderne" style informed by the aesthetic of the new, streamlined automobile and oriented the store's main entrances toward two motor courts providing parking for six hundred cars. Shellhorn's landscape design transformed Becket's plan into a parklike oasis within a larger suburban landscape. She chose a relatively limited

Bullock's Pasadena, 1947. Photograph by Julius Shulman. Courtesy © J. Paul Getty Trust. Getty Research Institute, Los Angeles (2004.R.10).

plant palette in keeping with the size and simplicity of the architecture.[2]

The planting plan for Bullock's Pasadena was guided by Winnett and defined by what he did not want—"nothing 'Eastern' looking!"[3] Shellhorn interpreted Winnett's directive by excluding deciduous plants and introducing subtropical varieties with brilliant, profuse blooming habits. After selecting plants that could adapt to the hot, dry summers and

Bullock's Pasadena, 1947. Photograph by Julius Shulman. Courtesy © J. Paul Getty Trust. Getty Research Institute, Los Angeles (2004.R.10).

cold, wet winters of the interior valley, she looked for shiny leaves, striking shapes, and rich textures. Groupings of tall Mexican fan palms with feathery leaves and lemon-scented gum trees with graceful, drooping branches fit these criteria.

Winnett's admonishment was uppermost in Shellhorn's mind when it came time to select a plant for acres of ground-cover. She wanted something "shining and tropical-looking." Driving down Huntington Drive one day, she spotted Algerian ivy covering a fence and envisioned the wind rippling over its fast-growing, glossy leaves. With Bullock's management's approval, she arranged to have Wilcox Nursery in nearby Montebello grow the ivy for her in flats. Later, she laughingly acknowledged the misuse and overuse of ivy, but continued to maintain that, properly used, it was an excellent choice. "Now it's all over, everywhere . . . and it's a pest. But for its purpose, it was good." Shellhorn also adapted star jasmine, another plant more commonly seen as a vine, for use as a bushy groundcover and had it grown by Hines Nursery in Altadena. She valued the fine texture and dainty white flowers of this slower-growing plant for pedestrian areas and used it frequently in planters along walkways and parking bays.[4]

Concerned that the Pasadena store might appear to overwhelm its site, Shellhorn carefully modulated plant textures to help mitigate this possibility. At the front of the store facing Lake Avenue, she experimented with graduated leaf sizes to create a sense of depth. The larger leaves of Algerian ivy in the foreground and the finer textures of sago palm and Senegal date palm in the background accentuated the distance from the street. Her carefully composed vignette for the front entrance achieved the illusion of depth with the feathery texture of Senegal date palm and a dark massing of laurel-leaf snailseed, which was intended to "hold the build-

Passageway between store and parking structure, 1985. Photograph by Robert M. Fletcher. Courtesy Burton and Patricia Fletcher.

Bullock's Pasadena, 1985. Photograph by Robert M. Fletcher. Courtesy Burton and Patricia Fletcher.

ing down."[5] Acres of shimmering Algerian ivy rippled in the wind, adding drama to the large expanse, which sloped down to the main boulevard.

Shellhorn understood that most shoppers would arrive by car and designed their first impression to be as attractive as the pedestrian entrance. She presented arriving customers with lavishly planted parking areas, ivy-covered embankments, evergreen shrubbery, and graceful trees with spreading canopies. Customers knew immediately that they were "parking in a park."[6] Achieving the desired look required a large number of specimen trees, many of which were unavailable from nurseries so soon after the war. Shellhorn's search for full-grown magnolia trees and phoenix palms began in 1945, just as the landscape design got under way. She prepared sketches illustrating the sizes and shapes she had in mind, and it took tree scouts almost a year to locate magnolia trees to her specifications. After she approved each of the trees, she had them boxed by Wilcox Nursery and held for later planting.[7] The trees thrived in the parking area's reflected asphalt heat, providing shade and a visual marker for each of the parking bays. When a multilevel parking structure replaced the open parking terrace in 1957, Shellhorn had these prized magnolias reboxed and moved to Bullock's Fashion Square Santa Ana.

The back of the Bullock's Pasadena property ran parallel to a residential neighborhood on Hudson Avenue. Shellhorn recognized the need for harmony with the existing scale and flora of the single-family residences, but she also wanted this sensitive interface zone to express a distinctive character. She widened the sidewalks to create a more spacious approach to the store and planted a rhythmic, uniformly spaced row of carob trees in wide beds of the same glistening Algerian ivy.[8] Because the cadence of the trees was a critical element of her

View of entrance on Lake Avenue, c. 1948. Photograph by Maynard Parker. Courtesy The Huntington Library, San Marino, CA.

plan, the "planters were designed down to the inch, so the symmetry was even."[9] The inspiration for this arrangement came from seeing palm trees lined up behind rows of lower trees in a 1945 *March of Time* newsreel on Palestine.[10] The carob trees, which were shaped to almost identical proportions, were also in scale with the street trees on the opposite side of Hudson Avenue.

In contrast to the street facade, views to the back of the store and the parking terraces featured colorful flora. Red trumpet vine grew on the fence, giving way to red hibiscus against the fieldstone wall. Espaliered loquat spread horizontally, following the lines of the stone. On the interior side of the Lake Avenue motor court, bougainvillea cascaded over both sides of the wall. Shellhorn alternated between magenta bougainvillea and espaliers of hot-pink hibiscus that were contract-grown by the Evans & Reeves nursery two years before installation. The bright shots of color, along with Senegal date palm, sago palm, agapanthus, and Natal plum, transformed the otherwise featureless parking area into a lush enclosure. Shellhorn likened the contrast she created between the textured green front

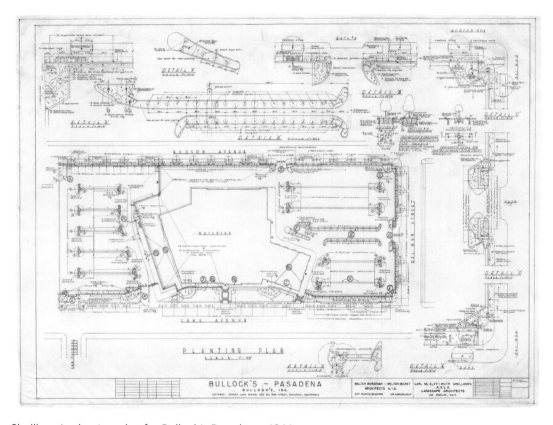

Shellhorn's planting plan for Bullock's Pasadena, 1946. Courtesy RSP.

of the store and the abundance of color in the back to a respectable, well-made coat with a festively patterned lining. Bronze-leaved plants provided a transition between areas, and the polished leaves of water vine adorned an alcove at the store entrance, adding a gleam of elegance as the door opened.[11]

Shellhorn guided drivers onto the north parking terrace between a double row of brilliant orange-flowering bird-of-paradise shrubs, alternating with small kumquat trees. The prospect of leaning out of the car window to pick the dangling citrus from these winter-fruiting trees delighted customers. Under the trees, she created a color planting by working out "a combination of blue and white petunias, pale yellow to orange zinnias for summer, and blue and white violas, and cream yellow and orange calendulas for winter."[12] The symmetrical structure of the plantings directed attention to the store entrance, which was framed with an asymmetrical composition of vertical Mexican fan palms, clumping Mediterranean fan palms, and giant bird-of-paradise. Tangerine-colored bougainvillea climbed up a stone wall and a cup-of-gold vine trailed over a nearby fence.[13] When it opened to the public in September 1947, Bullock's Pasadena was hailed as the "Store of Tomorrow." The first modern department store in the region to be located in the suburbs, it was also one of the first designed under the assumption that shoppers would arrive in automobiles. Everything about this new Bullock's spoke to a fresh, innovative style of California living.[14]

Shellhorn later designed and supervised the landscape plans for Bullock's Pasadena Tea Room Terrace, added in 1948, and a parking structure for 1,800 cars, built to replace the south parking lot in 1957. She consulted on long-term maintenance of the property until 1980. Bullock's Pasadena was listed on the National Register of Historic Places in 1996 and became part of a new shopping redevelopment in May 2002. Vestiges of Shellhorn's work include frontage plantings on Lake Street and remnants of the perimeter planting of carob trees on Hudson Avenue.

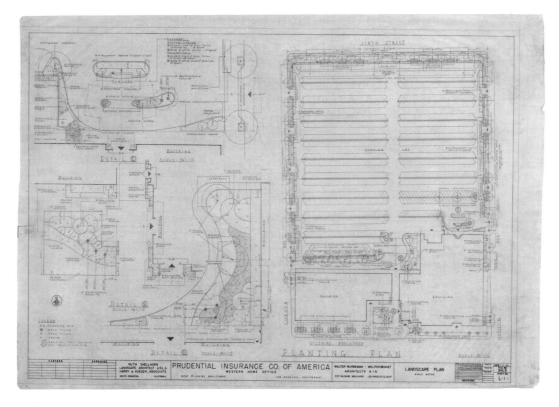

Shellhorn's landscape plan for Prudential Square, April 1948. Courtesy RSP.

PRUDENTIAL INSURANCE COMPANY OF AMERICA, WESTERN HOME OFFICE

LOS ANGELES, CALIFORNIA

1947–1957, OPENED 1948

In January 1947 the architect Walter Wurdeman, whose firm had worked with Shellhorn on the Bullock's Pasadena project, recommended her to his friends Mr. and Mrs. Henry Salvatori, who were seeking a landscape architect to create a design for their home in Bel-Air. Shellhorn got the job, and then successfully enlisted the Salvatoris' help in obtaining the commission for the landscape of an important Wurdeman & Becket building, the Prudential Insurance Western Home Office. By the end of the year, Shellhorn and her husband, Harry Kueser, had spent over a week building a model of the project, which would become Prudential Square.[1]

Part of the Wilshire Boulevard "Miracle Mile" in midtown Los Angeles, Prudential Square was bounded by Sixth Street on the north, Curson Avenue on the west, and Masselin Avenue on the east. Becket's International Style complex featured a ten-story central tower with a mezzanine and penthouse. The tower connected two ten-story office wings

Installation of Washington palm trees, 1948. Photograph by Ruth Shellhorn. In the author's possession.

West wing, 1949. Photograph by Douglas M. Simmonds. In the author's possession.

set back from the sidewalk. Most of the office space was taken up by Prudential, but an Ohrbach's department store leased a mezzanine and three floors behind the east wing, which was adjacent to a convenient parking lot at the back of the property. A single story of small shops extended along the front of the western wing. On Wilshire Boulevard, the buildings formed a large central L-shaped open space that extended back into the property from the sidewalk. Shellhorn turned this entrance court into an inviting garden. She specified Washington palms as a significant element in her planting scheme, placing them in twos and threes silhouetted against the central tower. A trio of these became the nucleus of a central planting group, anchored by the sculptural form of a giant bird-of-paradise on axis with the lobby doors. These were complemented by two palms near the south tower wall and two specimen magnolia trees flanking the entrance. She surrounded the trees with lower shrubs, including cocculus and hibiscus, using Algerian ivy as a groundcover.[2]

The Prudential commission allowed Shellhorn to experiment with a variety of planting compositions related to her earlier work at Bullock's Pasadena. Although the building was in a slightly more temperate climate zone, it was also close to the La Brea tar pits, which introduced gas bubbles and tar into the sandy soil. This unique challenge caused her to run "around town getting pointers on planting."[3] For the all-glass entrance into the Prudential offices, Shellhorn designed planting beds on both sides of the glass, creating a sense of transparency. Japanese aralia, Natal plum, giant bird-of-paradise, shell ginger, and shrimp plant made a subtly textured foreground for the dramatic lobby plantings of dracaena and fiddle-leaf figs.

The wide setback along Wilshire Boulevard allowed Shellhorn to introduce an unusually lush street planting. Four single cocos palms, each planted in a broad panel filled with Algerian ivy, lined the sidewalk of the east wing. The long, graceful palm fronds filled the limited space between canopy and curb and gave pattern to the lower building mass. A three-foot pittosporum hedge along the edge of the planting panels nearest the street enhanced separation of pedestrians and vehicles. Shellhorn described it "as a dark base course for the building" that also created "a sense of garden

Courtyard planting, 1949. Photograph by Douglas M. Simmonds. In the author's possession.

for the shops along the strip."[4] Planter boxes were used to continue the dark line of the hedge from the sidewalk to the eastern edge of the property, emphasizing the horizontal lines of the architecture.

As Shellhorn's 1947 and 1948 plans indicate, she paid careful attention to how plants could be combined in distinct compositions but also linked by a common theme. At the north tower wall, a grouping of Washington palms softened the height of the central tower. Two shrubby ficus trees marked the terminus of the entrance drive while adding a rich green base of planting to the long expanse of the west building. A hedge of Chinese holly was clipped to a five-foot height to separate the parking lot from the entrance drive. Groups of San Diego Red hibiscus were used for color and to build up mass at each end of the planting island.[5]

Entrance to tower, 1949. Photograph by Douglas M. Simmonds. In the author's possession.

Front courtyard, 1949. Photograph by Douglas M. Simmonds. In the author's possession.

Tower entrance from rear parking area, 1949. Photograph by Douglas M. Simmonds. In the author's possession.

In addition to Washington palm trees, lemon-scented gum trees were planted around the perimeter of the site for height and balance. These were underplanted with shrubs such as laurel-leaf snail tree, hibiscus, and xylosma and a groundcover of Algerian ivy. Planting along Sixth Street consisted of carob trees, prized for their dark green foliage and compact growth, and bays of white and pink oleander, Easter lily vine, and lawn. Shellhorn introduced more colorful flowering trees, shrubs, and espaliered vines in the interior of the parking lot and around the perimeter of the property. On Curson and Masselin Streets, she chose jacaranda trees, along with pink-blooming shrubs of Indian hawthorn accented by espaliered vines of gold Guinea flower, with yellow flowers in summer, pyracantha, with red berries in fall and winter, and blue sky flower through spring and fall. Her decision to bring color to the Prudential landscape design was similar to her plan for Bullock's Pasadena, but here we see a far greater variety of plant choices, and the beginning of her use of drifts of color to flow throughout a project, an experiment she continued in her Bullock's Fashion Square and campus projects.

Shellhorn also planned the landscape of an auxiliary parking area built on the other side of Masselin Avenue in 1949. After Becket designed a ten-story wing north of the central tower in 1955, Shellhorn redesigned the rear parking

Shellhorn receiving the American Association of Nurserymen's national "Plant America" award, 1955. In the author's possession.

area. That year she was recognized for her work on the Prudential project, winning the American Association of Nurserymen's "Plant America" Award.[6] The property underwent extensive remodeling in 1970 and now operates as Museum Square. Patio dining outside the west-wing shops has replaced the ivy and palms along Wilshire Boulevard, and the entrance court is now entirely paved over, but many of the perimeter palms, ficus, and other trees remain.

KNAPP GARDEN

BRENTWOOD, LOS ANGELES

1948

In 1948 Shellhorn's colleague Fred Barlow recommended her to architect Roland Coate, who needed a landscape architect for one of his residential commissions, the home and studio of the artist Edith Knapp. The property was located in Brentwood, a wealthy residential neighborhood in the Westside area of Los Angeles about five miles from the Pacific Ocean. Situated on a narrow lot, the house was approached up a driveway that curved around three old oak trees before terminating at a large motor court in front of the entrance. A row of mature poplar trees bordered the property's eastern edge. Coate had sited the simple two-story stucco structure to take advantage of views of the Santa Monica Mountains to the west and the ocean to the south. In the late 1940s, the neighborhood was still relatively undeveloped and offered middle-ground views of chaparral-covered canyon.

In her consultation with Shellhorn, Knapp requested a private patio off her art studio and a public one off the living room for entertaining. Preserving views of the scenery beyond the garden was of utmost importance to her. Shellhorn gave the sweeping panorama due acknowledgment with two circular patios linked by a brick terrace that wrapped around the house. To further emphasize the surrounding landscape, she designed an innovative glass screen to protect guests from up-canyon winds and invite appreciation of the view. Shellhorn described herself as "a firm believer

Entrance drive, 1950. Photograph by Ruth Shellhorn. In the author's possession.

Windscreen with views of Santa Monica Mountains, 1950. Photograph by Ruth Shellhorn. In the author's possession.

in the preservation of natural beauty wherever possible, and working with the topography rather than against it." She went on to say that "although it is often more difficult to do this, and it takes more time and thought, a much more individual and interesting effect will be achieved. . . . The homeowner here wanted the view afforded by this hilltop but not the wind. Glass set in redwood framing permitted fulfillment of both desires."[1] A white-flowering peach anchored the scene, providing spring flowers and summer shade. Shellhorn created a colorful, textured foreground for the windscreen using succulents, including agave, aloe, and white-flowering sedum as a groundcover. The shade border against the house included orange and coral fuchsias, camellias, and azaleas.[2]

The private studio patio on the north was separated from the motor court with a rustic redwood fence and gate. A large existing elderberry framed views and cast shade over a composition of dark green shrubs that included aralia, cocculus, viburnum, coral bells, and columbine. In the shade of the north-facing studio windows Shellhorn planted acanthus, camellias, and grape ivy. Sunny areas of the patio featured the warm yellow, orange, flame, and coral colors of daylily, sedum, aeonium, and heavenly bamboo. The brick paving contrasted with the varied green textures of oscularia and sedum, and velvety rosettes of echeveria punctuated clusters of aeonium in a fine-textured path edging.[3]

In addition to the winding entrance drive, a meandering pedestrian path gave access from the street to the motor court. Shellhorn's desire to balance the surrounding scenery with non-native plants near the house prompted a rustic step design with rough timbers for risers, redwood rounds sunk in the ground between for treads, and stabilized decomposed granite for the path. She tied these elements together with

Patio and windscreen, 1949. Photograph by Maynard L. Parker. Courtesy The Huntington Library, San Marino, CA.

contrasting groundcover patterns of creeping thyme and native strawberries.[4]

Shellhorn considered the vegetation beyond the edge of the property, such as indigenous oak, sycamore, sumac, elderberry, and ceanothus, a determining factor in her choice of perimeter plants. She finely tuned her planting plan to

ERNEST BRAUN

MAYNARD L. PARKER

Entry to studio patio *from motor court.
Private with gate closed. Aloe, iceplant,
at left; banana, rice paper plant beyond*

Studio patio *off north end of house is joined to "entertaining patio" by brick walk.
Acanthus, camellias, and grape ivy in bed under studio windows. Aralia, cocculus,
viburnum, coral bells, and columbine in shade planting under elderberry on the right*

One generous patio for entertaining ... another

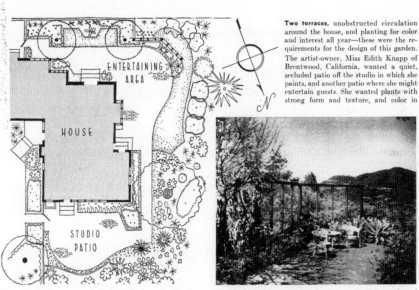

Two terraces, unobstructed circulation
around the house, and planting for color
and interest all year—these were the requirements for the design of this garden.
The artist-owner, Miss Edith Knapp of
Brentwood, California, wanted a quiet,
secluded patio off the studio in which she
paints, and another patio where she might
entertain guests. She wanted plants with
strong form and texture, and color in

Plan *shows how space around the house has been developed to
provide generous living and entertaining areas and continuous
circulation. Motor court in front and service in rear not shown*

View *of Santa Monica Mountains from entertaining patio and
living room. Glass wall breaks wind, mirrors color of planting
in front, and lets you look through to the green plants beyond*

Plan and photos of the Knapp garden, 1955. Courtesy *Sunset Magazine.*

interweave these native plants with compatible non–native species, such as Brazilian pepper, cotoneaster, pyracantha, cocculus, and oleander. Around the perimeter of the property, these plantings softened the transition between the chaparral and the domestic greenery, gradually becoming lusher around the house. The front garden included two areas of lawn and a composition of bauhinia and magnolia trees, as well as three different varieties of banana trees.

North-facing art studio patio, 1949. Photograph by Maynard L. Parker. Courtesy The Huntington Library, San Marino, CA.

Windscreen, looking south, 1952. Photograph by Ruth Shellhorn. Courtesy RSP.

Shellhorn visited the Knapp property four to six times a year for almost two decades to review the progress of the garden and write detailed maintenance instructions. Neighboring development eventually blocked much of the view, and the house and garden were subsequently demolished.[5]

DISNEYLAND

In March 1955, construction crews were working seven days a week to complete Walt Disney's new theme park before its scheduled opening in July. As construction rapidly progressed, Disney worried that the project might not "hang together." He was in urgent need of a landscape architect to unify the distinctive elements of Adventureland, Frontierland, Fantasyland, and Tomorrowland into a coherent whole. A friend, the architect Welton Becket, recommended only Ruth Shellhorn.[1]

Shellhorn immediately understood the potential qualities of the site and began working out hardscape plans and planting details for the front entrance, Town Square, and Main Street. A comprehensive pedestrian plan for the entire park quickly followed, along with an innovative planting scheme for the central Plaza Hub garden located in front of Sleeping Beauty Castle. Designing in the field without plans, she helped lay out watercourses with stakes and string

Aerial view of Disneyland, 1955. In the author's possession.

and supervised grading around the moat to dramatize the park's centerpiece, the majestic castle. Under Disney's direction, she worked alongside the art directors as part of an elite leadership team of otherwise male designers who oversaw design of the park. Her engineering skills became apparent when she discovered discrepancies in grades and dimensions that were appreciatively acknowledged by surprised road crews.[2]

All of the major structures and attractions in the park were in various stages of construction and fixed in terms of location when Shellhorn began work on the project. Disneyland covered 160 acres, including approximately 68 acres devoted to concentrated areas of development, and its site resembled an inverted triangle with rounded corners. Surrounded by a fifteen-foot-high raised berm, the park was completely enclosed with thickly planted trees and shrubs to create horizon points, frame internal views, and obscure views into and outside of the park. Ticket booths and twin entrances through two low tunnels greeted visitors at the southern apex of the triangle.[3] Shellhorn later described the layout of the project in an article she wrote for *Landscape Architecture* in 1956. "From the Railway Station at the entrance

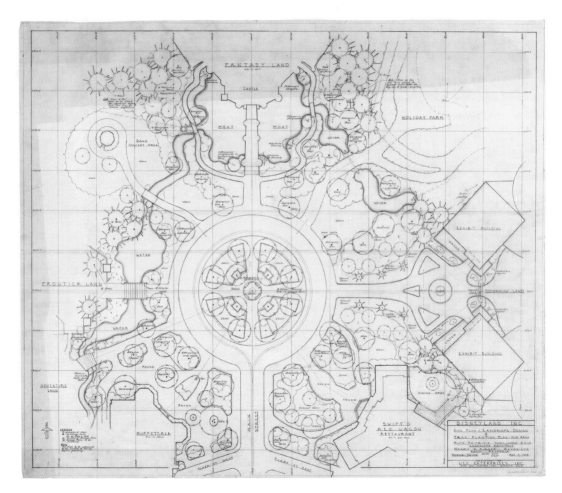

"Site Plan—Landscape Design & Tree Planting Plan—Hub Area," May 7, 1955. Courtesy RSP.

the view extends north across the Town Square and down Main Street to the Hub of the Plaza, beyond which Sleeping Beauty Castle terminates the vista. From the Hub walks radiate to the other four main divisions of Disneyland. . . . Tomorrowland, the realm of the future, lies to the east. . . . Frontierland, occupying the northwest third of the park, with its New Orleans section, the Rivers of America, and the Painted Desert, is the largest section. . . . Tropical Adventureland, with its Rivers of the World, lies in the southwest section. . . . Fantasyland, at the north central portion of the scheme, is approached through the Castle itself."[4]

The existing program for the park's pedestrian circulation plan thus offered Shellhorn limited options. Her challenge was to optimize the use of space between the different elements so that crowds could move smoothly, while main-

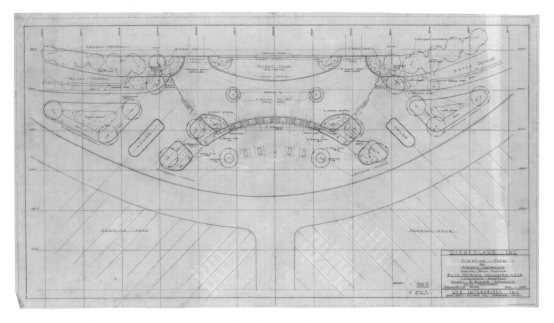

"Planting Plan for Front Entrance Showing Tree Planting," June 1, 1955. Courtesy RSP.

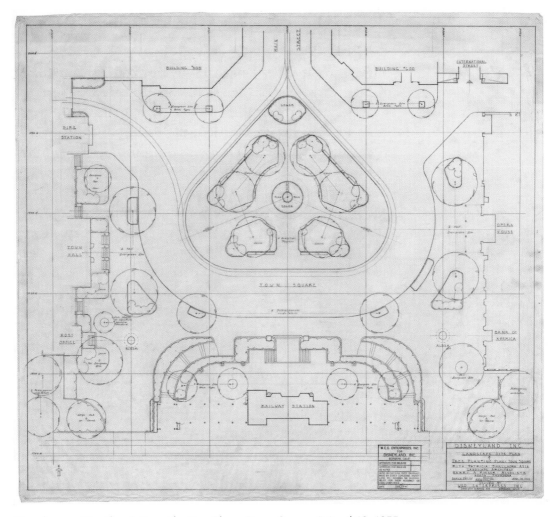

"Landscape Site Plan & Tree Planting Plan—Town Square," April 18, 1955. Courtesy RSP.

taining a sense of suspense by not revealing too much at one time. To guide the arrival and movement of visitors from the entrance to Sleeping Beauty Castle, park designers employed the principle of "progressive realization," highlighting the visual experience by gradually introducing the featured element.[5] Using strategically placed groupings of trees, Shell-horn concealed and revealed the vista of the castle as visitors arrived at the ticket booth, lingered in the Town Square, or strolled along Main Street to reach the Plaza Hub. She relied on the careful shaping, sizing, and positioning of planted areas to control pedestrian movement. She narrowed walk-ways to quicken and direct movement, expanded "pause points" to allow for a momentary rest stop or change of di-rection, and split traffic around planting islands to minimize congestion near attractions.[6]

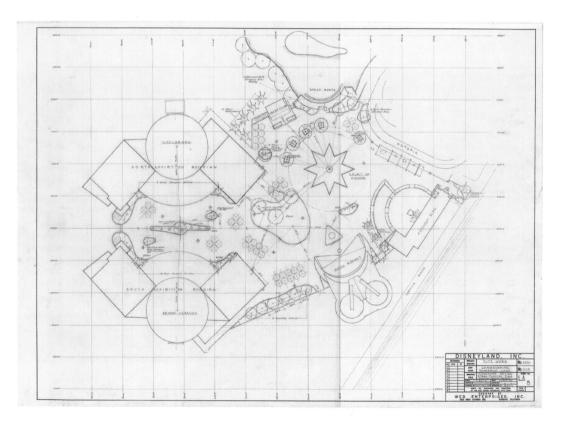

"Landscape Design and Tree Planting Plan, Showing Paving Layout, Tomorrowland," June 25, 1955.
Courtesy RSP.

From the first day of planning, Walt Disney required that Disneyland be of the highest "show" quality. He called for an aesthetic and philosophical approach in the planting design that would realize his childhood yearning for "Eternal Spring," with as much color as possible and the largest specimen trees available. These were procured by the landscape architects Jack and Morgan "Bill" Evans, both of whom brought superior horticultural experience to the project. During the previous two years, the Evans brothers had been collecting specimen trees, many of them rescued

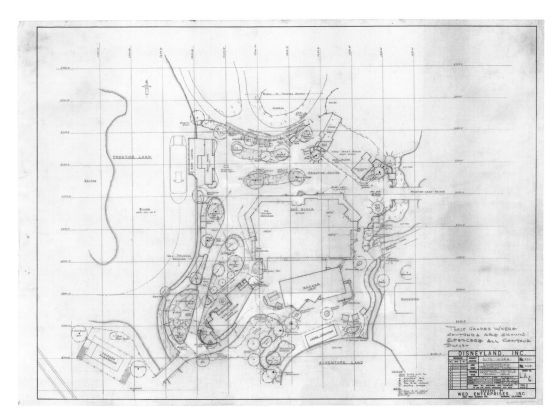

"Landscaping Frontierland & Adventureland—Landscape Design & Tree Planting Plan—Central Areas," May 28, 1955. Courtesy RSP.

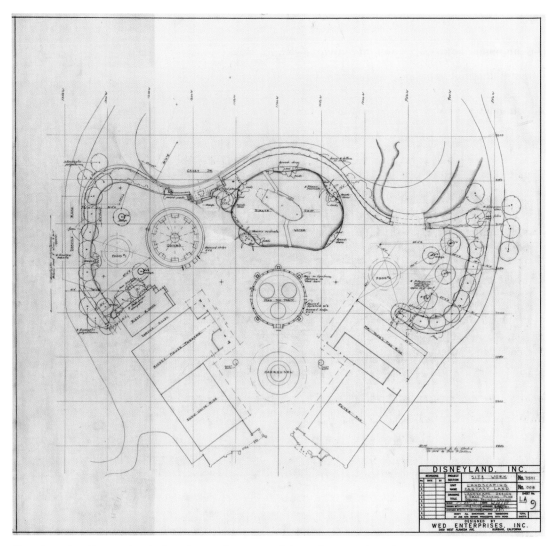

"Landscaping Fantasyland—Landscape Design and Tree Planting Plan Showing Paving Layout," June 30, 1955. Courtesy RSP.

Adventureland art director Harper Goff, landscape architect Bill Evans, and head director Dick Irvine with Walt Disney, Shellhorn, and construction chief Joe Fowler, April 1955. Photograph by Harry Kueser. Courtesy RSP.

from the bulldozer as new freeways and suburban development spread throughout the region. They moved, planted, and maintained major trees all over the site and installed a dense landscape screen on the perimeter. Shellhorn worked closely with them in tasks big and small, helping to identify key botanical elements for each area among the small forest of specimen trees they amassed on the site and even to create a rotating palette for the enormous floral portrait of Mickey Mouse adjacent to the ticket booth. She suggested bright seasonal annuals, such as dwarf pink phlox for Mickey's tongue.[7]

Town Square was intended to provide a nostalgic look at old-time America. Visitors proceeding from the ticket booth entered an open-air plaza filled with Victorian-era

The bandstand was replaced with a flagpole, as originally intended, May 14, 1955. Photograph by Ruth Shellhorn. Courtesy RSP.

Olive trees in the Plaza Hub were placed during construction of Sleeping Beauty Castle, May 14, 1955. Photograph by Ruth Shellhorn. Courtesy RSP.

bustle and gilded decor. Horse-drawn wagons circled a small park in the center of the square. Shellhorn first created a sense of enclosure, setting Chinese elm trees with "character" around the perimeter of the square and two mature Victorian boxwood trees on either side of the railway station. Because the area had to be quite large to accommodate the crowds, park designers built the 1890s-style architecture and trains at 5/8 scale to help diminish the sense of an oversized space. Shellhorn created areas for quiet retreat that encouraged visitors to focus on planting and architectural details and also helped to normalize the scale of the square. In the central circle she placed small, inviting patches of green lawn just the right size for a family to stop and rest. She chose formally pruned Brazilian pepper trees to cast shade over benches set in from the sidewalks, away from pedestrian traffic. To embellish Disney's patriotic theme, she specified reddish concrete paving, white-flowering trees and shrubs, and flowering groundcovers and perennials in shades of red, white, and blue. An old cannon completed the scene of small-town America.[8]

The scale of the Town Square and its modulation became one of the few points of disagreement between Shellhorn and Disney. The original studio drawings for the central island showed a flagpole in the center. In a burst of enthusiasm, Disney decided to replace the flagpole with a bandstand. Shellhorn protested that it was too big for the space and interfered with the pedestrian sight line from the Town Square to the castle. Halfway through construction, Disney came back to take a look, decided he agreed with Shellhorn, and ordered the bandstand out. He learned to trust her judgment; just two months after she joined the project, he declared, "I have absolute confidence in your ability."[9]

As pedestrians were funneled from Town Square to

Shellhorn directing placement of a holly oak tree in front of the main entrance, May 25, 1955. Photograph by Harry Kueser. Courtesy RSP.

Main Street, numerous shops and attractions increased the tempo of activity. Shellhorn delineated views from the Town Square entrance down Main Street to the castle with a double row of Chinese elm trees. Selected by Jack Evans for a uniform appearance, the elms contributed architectural structure, enhanced a sense of enclosure, and provided a respite from the summer sun. Shellhorn painstakingly adjusted the placement of the trees so that they would not obstruct entrances to buildings, but her highest priority was to frame views and create a consistent cadence in leading pedestrians up to the Plaza Hub at the base of the castle.

Shellhorn directing grading for the bulldozers carving a moat around Sleeping Beauty Castle, six weeks before opening day, June 6, 1955. Photograph by Harry Kueser. Courtesy RSP.

In the Plaza Hub, visitors sat beneath the shade of seventy-five-year-old olive trees and paused to admire the object of their journey. Sleeping Beauty Castle, flanked on either side by enormous earthen berms, was anchored with a thickly planted background of what would become towering pine and cedar trees. Shellhorn specified that the trees be planted in drifts, making the castle seem to emerge from a deep, dark forest.[10] Canary Island pine was substituted for the Northern European fir and spruce trees that surrounded Neuschwanstein Castle in Germany, the likely model for Disney's theme park palace.[11]

For the Plaza Hub, Shellhorn was charged with designing a 360-degree garden landscape that would unify the dissimilar environments represented by the entrances to a dusty western frontier, a tropical jungle, a vision of childhood fantasy, and a glimpse into the future. But ecological reality did not permit the wholesale transport of entire plant communities to the hot, dry climate and silty soil of Anaheim, California. Under the direction of Jack Evans, the landscape workforce amended acres of soil and installed miles of irrigation pipeline.[12] This infrastructure made it possible for Shellhorn to reinterpret the character of those landscapes by substituting plants that were similarly distinctive but could also tolerate the site conditions. Most visitors never realized that each land's entrance was subtly identified by its own botanical signature, or that the landscape along the pedestrian paths leading to each land held clues to what lay beyond.

Shellhorn placed a middle ground of Australian tea tree

Walt Disney playfully shooting a "gun" during a meeting with Shellhorn and the art directors, June 4, 1955. Photograph by Ruth Shellhorn. Courtesy RSP.

and flowering pear into the sweep of the surrounding garden. She was allowed to introduce a few deciduous trees, such as flowering peach and crepe myrtle, for variety of color and texture, but only in limited numbers. Walt Disney was adamant about minimizing plantings that, in dormancy, might recall an image of cold weather. She responded with a panoramic display of "Eternal Spring"—evergreen trees such as fern pine for its fine texture, Indian laurel for its shining green color, and Italian stone pine for its rugged character. She wove the scene together with a foreground of colorful shrubs, flowering annuals and perennials, and the finely textured greens of a variety of junipers. Within this tapestry, Shellhorn helped lay out paths and footbridges that crisscrossed streams adjacent to the castle, specifying groupings of rocks to anchor the planting vignettes.

Surrounding the castle was a moat inhabited by black and white swans. Shellhorn edged the moat with juniper,

Ruth Shellhorn and Walt Disney at Western Railway station two weeks before opening day, July 2, 1955. Photograph by Harry Kueser. In the author's possession.

Town Square with flagpole, 1987. Photograph by Robert M. Fletcher. Courtesy Burton and Patricia Fletcher.

which Morgan Evans called "swan-proof" because, in his experience, this was the only plant the swans would not eat.[13] Adjacent to the water's edge, Shellhorn planted graceful willow-leaf pittosporum trees to reflect in the still water and melaleuca to overhang the banks. The twisted, gnarly trunk and branch structure emphasized the sinister aspect of a secluded wood inhabited by an evil queen. At the same time, the melaleuca's fine, filmy foliage gave the space a fairylike quality, a fitting entrance to Fantasyland.[14]

North of the Plaza, a drawbridge led to Fantasyland through Sleeping Beauty Castle. The constructed elements left little vacant space for planting, but Shellhorn was still able to create a sense that the visitor was entering a different world. She delineated the perimeter of the seating and food service areas with eucalyptus, elm, and silk oak trees, provided shade with fern pine, and introduced a "spring" scent with mock orange and citrus trees.[15] Next to the Pirate Ship restaurant, Shellhorn created the impression of a tropical cove in just four pocket planters. "As every available square foot was needed for paving in this concentrated area of activity, little could be spared for planting," she noted. "Casey Jr. [a train ride] was prominent in the background, and the Tea Cup Ride in the foreground. . . . [A] desert island was suggested by the simple expedient of using beach sand with

Senegal date palms adjacent to the Pirate Ship in Fantasyland, 1955. In the author's possession.

clumps of reeds and Senegal [date] palms placed strategically around the edge of the water."[16]

To the west of the Plaza Hub, the entrance to Frontierland included a log stockade accessed by a path with a rough-hewn wooden bridge crossing over a stream. Shellhorn framed the entrance with California native plants, including strawberry tree, lemonade berry, Oregon grape, and ceanothus, but also employed non-native plants with rugged forms. One of the planting characteristics she identified for Frontierland was a "mountain feeling," with "isolated" pine trees to express the aridity and desolation of the Old West.[17] Her drawings specified Japanese black pine, with its contorted, windblown appearance, along with trees featuring gnarled trunks and textured bark, such as Australian tea tree and melaleuca. To emphasize the natural appearance of this area, she planted vines, currant, pennisetum, and several varieties of ceanothus to spill along the banks of the stream, requested tumbled rocks with branches lodged up against the bridge, and strategically placed fountain grass at the water's edge.[18]

Shellhorn described the entrance to Adventureland as one of her most complicated challenges, "due to its close proximity to two completely different styles of architecture." The path leading from the Plaza Hub was bounded on the left by the Victorian-style Buffeteria restaurant and, on the right, by a stream that ran past the stockade and blockhouses of Frontierland. Shellhorn finessed the blending of this section by using "rough grasses" for the edge of the Frontierland side and creating a partial screen with grasslike bamboo. She also included "Senegal date palm, jacaranda, and bougainvillea, often found in the gardens of early Victorian houses in California," which offered tropical bursts of purple and magenta in the approach to Adventureland. To convey the

Sleeping Beauty Castle from the Plaza Hub, 1963. Photograph by William Aplin. Courtesy Collections of the Los Angeles County Arboretum and Botanic Garden.

A contorted melaleuca at the edge of the moat around Sleeping Beauty Castle, 1987. Photograph by Robert M. Fletcher. Courtesy Burton and Patricia Fletcher.

jungle motif framing the portal to Adventureland, Shellhorn used a combination of tropical plants selected by the Evans brothers. Canary Island date palms and coconut palms swayed in the background, merging with Senegal date palms and other broad-leafed subtropical plants, such as xylosma, philodendron, and melianthus.[19]

Tomorrowland presented a quite different landscape design puzzle. Without an existing model to consult, Shellhorn drew on modernist design elements and a large vocabulary of plants associated with contemporary landscapes. Her drawings featured planting areas in abstract shapes and emphasized the use of plants with strong geometric forms and bold colors.[20] She broadened the entrance walk leading east into Tomorrowland from the Plaza Hub so that it flared into a pentagon-shaped courtyard, and lined the path with regimented Italian cypress that marched forward in monochromatic beds of English ivy. The vertical shapes of the cypress trees referred to the rocket ship up ahead, forever poised for launch into space.

To emphasize entrances to rides, Shellhorn made room for dramatic clumps of Senegal date palm, Hollywood juniper, and bird-of-paradise, as well as bedding plants in blasts of color. Visitors approaching the Clock of the World, a futuristic conical tower that told the time in twenty-four time zones, found it "perpetually encircled by flowers: the rich orange of French marigolds in spring, petunias in summer, lavender vinca in fall, and violas in winter."[21] In a playful, backward reference to air travel, Shellhorn inserted a central planting bed in the shape of a propeller, recalling the prop engine planes soon to be supplanted by jets.

While each of the lands exhibited a characteristic theme and plant palette, Disney's grand vision required a sense of harmonious continuity throughout the park. To maintain the spell of enchantment, Shellhorn employed the same technique she used in unifying landscape vignettes at the Plaza Hub, but on a larger scale. The most skillful of these transitions occurred in moving from the stockades of Frontierland through the gingerbread architecture of New Orleans Square to the tiki huts of Adventureland. Shellhorn specified drifts of white-flowering trees or shrubs, beginning with melaleuca, then oleander, then magnolia, and ending with citrus. She interwove the whole sequence with evergreen oak, flowering pear, and elm trees. Her composition made the areas flow together so seamlessly that visitors were unaware of her artistic intervention.[22]

Ten years after Disneyland opened, Walt Disney expressed his personal appreciation to Shellhorn for her special role in creating "the happiest place on earth."[23] Even while Disneyland continues to evolve and expand, the imprint of Shellhorn's core landscape design remains intact, serving as an enduring and highly imaginative example of her public work.

UNIVERSITY OF CALIFORNIA, RIVERSIDE

LANDSCAPE MASTER PLAN AND ASSOCIATED PROJECTS

1956–1964

In 1954 the University of California system opened a small liberal arts college on the outskirts of Riverside, set near the Santa Ana River about sixty miles east of Los Angeles. The college joined an existing state-run citrus experiment station, and in 1960 the joint facility became a full-fledged university in the UC system.[1]

Almost as soon as it opened the school began to grow, and in 1956 Shellhorn was selected as supervising landscape architect to design and oversee construction of new landscape projects on the expanding campus. Her position included responsibility for all areas of landscape design—the location of roads, walks, lighting, and utilities, as well as new planting throughout the campus. She would serve in this role for eight years, creating a variety of designed landscapes as she collaborated on a master plan over which she exerted considerable influence.

The natural beauty of the site inspired Shellhorn. Set at

the base of the Box Springs Mountains, the campus gently sloped up from citrus groves to blend into the rocky foothills. Eucalyptus, palm, and citrus trees, remnants of the university's roots as an agricultural facility, formed a rich tapestry of green against the hills. Shellhorn saw "a wealth of possibilities" in the rugged site "traversed by canyons, *barrancas,* and draws with an infinite variety of character," and she

Aerial view of UC Riverside campus, c. 1956. Courtesy Special Collections & University Archives, UCR Library, University of California, Riverside.

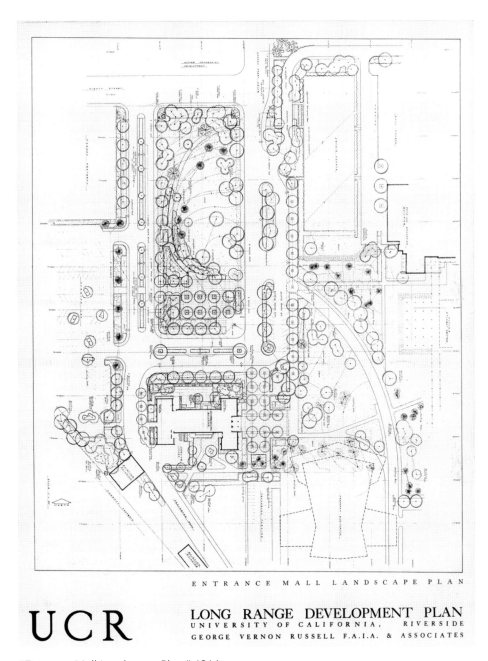

ENTRANCE MALL LANDSCAPE PLAN

UCR

LONG RANGE DEVELOPMENT PLAN
UNIVERSITY OF CALIFORNIA, RIVERSIDE
GEORGE VERNON RUSSELL F.A.I.A. & ASSOCIATES

"Entrance Mall Landscape Plan," 1964. Courtesy RSP.

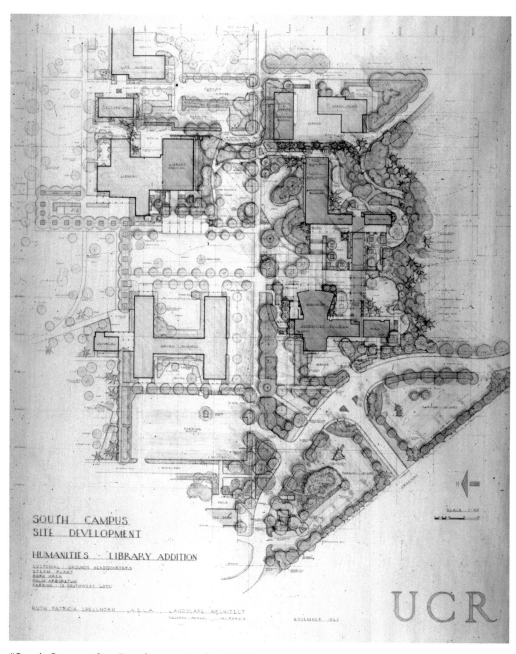

"South Campus Site Development" plan, 1964. Courtesy RSP.

Eucalyptus-lined path near Health Sciences building, 1987. Photograph by Robert M. Fletcher. Courtesy Burton and Patricia Fletcher.

was determined that her plan would emphasize its unique qualities.[2]

For years the administration had been considering filling in the arroyos to gain space for parking and athletic fields.[3] When Shellhorn arrived, she argued for the preservation of the area's distinctive natural features, and she found an authoritative ally in 1959, when the Pasadena-based architect George Vernon Russell was hired to assume a leadership role in coordinating and supervising further campus development. Russell agreed with her and took a prominent role in promoting their shared point of view. Shellhorn's com-

Pedestrian bridge over arroyo near Health Sciences building, 2011. Photograph by Ruth Taylor Kilday. In the author's possession.

mitment to preserve the canyons led her to suggest the use of bridges, rather than fills and culverts, whenever possible.[4] For a wide mesa in the north campus occupied by the Health Sciences building, "one of the finest sites . . . [with] a view of the entire campus," she planned a bridge to the residence halls and a pedestrian bridge from the halls to the athletic field area.[5] She then created a winding pedestrian walkway across the canyon with a branch along the far side ending at

Carillon bell tower, 1966. Photograph by Ansel Adams. Courtesy California Museum of Photography.

Humanities building and Performing Arts Theater. Photograph by Ansel Adams. Courtesy California Museum of Photography.

Perimeter Road. Minimizing grading cuts was as important to her plan as minimizing fill. To preserve the rolling topography she moved the Health Sciences parking area, eliminating the need to make the deep cuts into the natural grade required for the earlier proposed location north of the building. In addition to their scenic value, the canyons provided opportunities for hiking trails, picnic grounds, an arboretum, and environmental study areas. Shellhorn also envisioned a small lake at the bottom of the Health Sciences canyon, although this distinctive feature fell victim to budget constraints.

Whenever possible, Shellhorn designed outdoor spaces to take advantage of the spectacular views. In the Long Range Development Plan prepared for the university in 1964, she

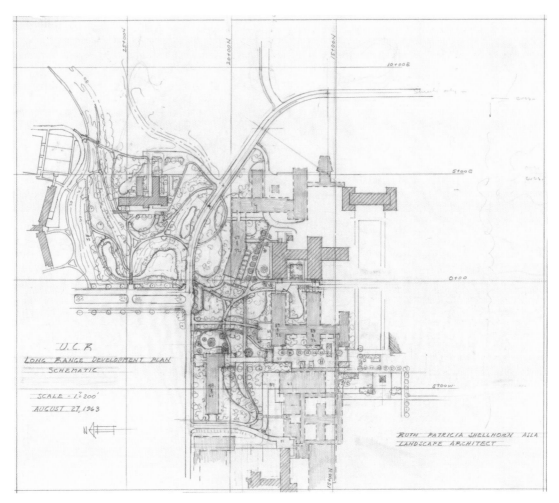

"Long Range Development Plan Schematic," August 27, 1963. Courtesy RSP.

wrote, "Rivers of green should flow between the buildings and courtyards, knitting them together, framing vistas, and forming a variety of spaces ranging from large open lawns to intimate gardens. Open areas or vistas framed by trees among the buildings will create a sense of distance in contrast with confined spaces." At Riverside, Shellhorn sought plants that would bring "the color of the hills" into the campus and contrast with the "cool, rich greens" of lawn and

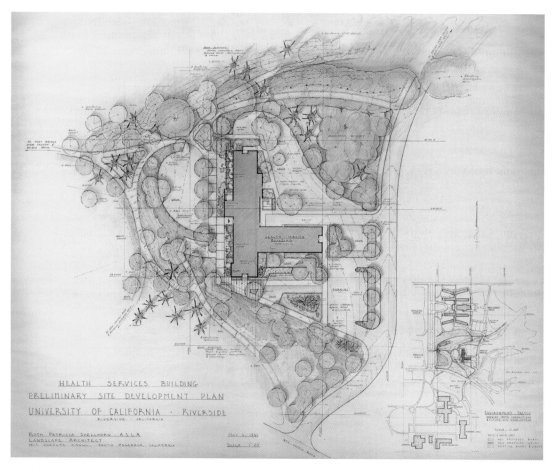

"Health Services [Sciences] Building, Preliminary Site Development Plan," May 6, 1961. Courtesy RSP.

Science building, 1964. Photograph by Julius Shulman. Courtesy © J. Paul Getty Trust. Getty Research Institute, Los Angeles (2004.R.10).

Science building, 1964. Photograph by Julius Shulman. Courtesy © J. Paul Getty Trust. Getty Research Institute, Los Angeles (2004.R.10).

tall shade trees. She continued to use a variety of non-native trees, such as olive and eucalyptus, which were remnants of previous planting schemes and blended with the chaparral of the surrounding landscape.[6]

Natural rock outcroppings prompted Shellhorn's use of rock in walls and paving, and in combination with plants to emphasize this aspect of the surrounding environment. In the Administration Plaza she ran ribbons of aggregate concrete, carefully tinted to harmonize with the landscape. Similar paving treatment extended to other areas of the campus to delineate seating areas. The washes of rock gravel in the adjacent canyons were suggested by the groundcover in the patio planting areas of the Administration building. Even the benches in the plaza, constructed with brick supports and

Science building, 1964. Photograph by Julius Shulman. Courtesy © J. Paul Getty Trust. Getty Research Institute, Los Angeles (2004.R.10).

wooden seats, were placed with one support in the planting well, illustrating, in a small way, an association with the natural setting.

All of Shellhorn's designs also considered Riverside's climate—triple-digit summer heat and below-freezing winter temperatures—as well as the Santa Ana winds that swept across the campus in fall and winter. At the Health Sciences building, a walkway led from the parking lot to a sitting area looking out over the campus and shaded by a lofty group of sycamore and olive trees. For the Administration Plaza, Shellhorn created a sunken garden thickly planted with deciduous Chinese flame trees. In spite of water considerations, Shellhorn didn't hesitate to choose more traditional plantings for selected areas. Large panels of lawn linked the main mall between Webber Hall and Hinderaker Hall. And Shellhorn indulged in a bit of whimsy in the entrance to campus, graduating the color of roses in the roadway median to "accelerate" from white to pale yellow, then to orange, and finishing with a brilliant red. Groundskeepers continued to

Administration building, north patio, 1976. Photograph by Ruth Shellhorn. Courtesy RSP.

View north from the Humanities building, 1966. Photograph by Ansel Adams. Courtesy California Museum of Photography.

maintain this scheme for many years, replanting spent roses with exactly the same colors chosen by Shellhorn and, in some cases, growing their own from cuttings.[7]

Shellhorn's plan for the Health Sciences area won the California Landscape Contractors Association's Trophy Award for Public Works in 1963. The university's *Long Range Development Plan*, published a year later, illustrates her most enduring contribution: creating a set of specific design guidelines to articulate and implement further development throughout the campus. Russell and Shellhorn's shared belief in the value of site-responsive design became a corner-stone of the plan, as did their statement about the intent of the landscape design guidelines. Both championed a scheme in which "building and landscape arrangements that might generate excessive monumentality have been deliberately avoided—this in the belief that intimate courts, connecting passages, gates and a variety of landscape features might create an environment where intellectual interchange and human relationships might be more easily propagated." In the development plan, Shellhorn synthesized components from her landscape architectural studies and projects, focusing on the overall layout as she considered possibilities that would best preserve the natural qualities of the site.[8]

In 1964, an increase in private commissions forced Shellhorn to consider either enlarging her office or continuing to maintain close control over her creative output, and she reluctantly resigned from her position at Riverside.[9] During her eight-year tenure, she had been directly responsible for plans or the supervision of plans at seventeen separate areas of the campus. All were completed in close cooperation with Russell and the university architect, R. J. Evans, and included supervision of the designs of executive landscape architects Arthur Barton, Yoshiro Befu, and Edward Huntsman-Trout. As the Riverside campus continues to expand, Shellhorn's influence and many of her landscape designs remain.

BULLOCK'S FASHION SQUARE SHOPPING CENTERS

LOS ANGELES AND ORANGE COUNTIES, CALIFORNIA

1956–1980

A few years after the opening of Bullock's Pasadena in 1947, company management noticed the growing number of related commercial developments in the vicinity and began planning an independent complex of fashion and home furnishings stores. The "controlled environment" concept, part of a nationwide trend in specialized development, prompted Bullock's to become its own real estate developer. The company not only bought land and erected structures for its own department stores, but also built and leased stores for merchants who might otherwise have been considered competitors. These tenants, preselected by Bullock's, sold high-quality apparel, home furnishings and accessories, and specialty goods and services.[1] Shellhorn created the landscape designs for the first four Bullock's Fashion Square shopping centers, in Santa Ana (1958), Sherman Oaks (1962), Torrance at Del Amo (1966), and La Habra (1968).

When Fashion Square Santa Ana opened in Orange

County in 1958 it was touted as the first planned shopping center of its kind in the United States. Bigger shopping malls and specialty store groupings had been built, but Fashion Square Santa Ana was the earliest integrated, specialty shopping complex in the country to employ a pedestrian mall as a unifying feature.[2] Shellhorn was responsible for the entire landscape design, which covered one-eighth of the fifty-acre project. The development included thirty-two stores built around a wide, central L-shaped mall with a fountain at one end and a rectangular pool at the other. A parking lot for 3,300 cars surrounded the buildings. Shellhorn had worked with only one architectural firm on each of three previous

Seating area at Fashion Square Del Amo, 1969. Photograph by Darrow M. Watt. Courtesy Sunset Publishing.

Bullock's department stores, but here she coordinated her landscape design with three firms. The new shopping center featured four anchor department stores: Bullock's, designed by Pereira & Luckman; Haggarty's and Desmond's, designed by Burke, Kober & Nicolais; and I. Magnin, designed by H. C. Chambers and Lester Hibbard.[3]

Having established her expertise in previous Bullock's commissions, Shellhorn was given an unusual amount of authority over the final design of the project. The lead architects, Pereira & Luckman, designed the preliminary landscape plan, which included a series of raised walkways about eighteen inches above grade. But Shellhorn envisioned a

South entrance of Fashion Square Santa Ana, 1969. Photograph by Darrow M. Watt. Courtesy Sunset Publishing.

linear greenway from Main Street all the way down the middle of the shopping center, and she convinced Bullock's management to let her redesign the mall.[4] Her overall goal, she said, was to evoke "'the California Atmosphere,' contemporary, yet reminiscent of an earlier, quieter, more romantic era." Her landscape plan was "designed to be quiet, restful, friendly and inviting with an abundance of soft green and accents of sparkling color in yellow flame and coral tones. The planting of the site is . . . rich and simple, with broad soft masses of material being used in keeping with the stately simplicity of the buildings."[5] She substituted at-grade concrete walkways, which visually receded in importance, and encapsulated plantings in overlapping squares and rectangles of low-profile aggregate concrete planters with smooth concrete caps, which served as impromptu seating. These changes emphasized the parklike qualities of the space and

Pots of agave and juniper, Fashion Square Del Amo, 1969. Photograph by Darrow M. Watt. Courtesy Sunset Publishing.

Brazilian pepper tree, Fashion Square Sherman Oaks, 1985. Photograph by Robert
M. Fletcher. Courtesy Burton and Patricia Fletcher.

Pool, Fashion Square Santa Ana, 1979. Photograph by the author.

acknowledged the aesthetic experience of the pedestrian shopper.[6]

Shellhorn's first priority for each Bullock's project was to visit the site and become familiar with its context, noting important views she wanted to enhance or screen and acquainting herself with the topography and existing flora. Describing these preliminary visits, Shellhorn said, "I let the site 'talk' to me, until I have a feeling for the area and its natural and manmade surroundings . . . I then try to create a design that restores or enlarges the possibilities of re-creating the natural setting. The design must blend with the setting yet be a unified landscape composition with the buildings."[7] Shellhorn's site-responsive method included her approach to plant selection, which became a matter of intense inquiry. She chose a color palette for each site, intuitively drawing on elements as ethereal as "the color of the air," or a chance scattering of weeds, as a basis for her selection. When she first visited the property that would be developed as Bullock's Fashion Square Santa Ana, for example, a sunny haze colored the sky and the landscape of orange groves over a sea of yellow oxalis. That scene inspired a "hot" color scheme of red-berried pepper trees, red-flowered bottlebrush trees, orange-blooming bird-of-paradise, and lemon-yellow hibiscus.[8]

By selecting major trees and shrubs that would relate to the surrounding neighborhood, Shellhorn expanded on her scheme of using the site's context as a source of inspiration. For Santa Ana, she incorporated nearby eucalyptus and palm trees, using these species to mark portions of the southern boundary and drift across the entire west area to create an informal skyline.[9] Along the northern perimeter of the site, she chose a stand of deodar cedars interspersed with California holly, a selection that referred to a fifty-year-old cedar found growing on the site when the shopping center was still on the drawing boards.[10] As with all the Bullock's projects, a signature trio of staggered Washington palm trees beckoned approaching shoppers to the store entrance.

One of Shellhorn's favorite methods for blending groups of trees within a site was to drift from one species to the next, approximating how she saw the growth of trees in nature. She said, "Nature doesn't group trees in exclusive colonies by types. One species drifts in among a group of other, a locust among oaks, for instance. I try for informality

Cup-of-gold vine and Guinea gold vine espaliers, Fashion Square La Habra, 1975. Photograph by Ruth Shellhorn. Courtesy RSP.

Entrance to Fashion Square Santa Ana, 1987. Photograph by Robert M. Fletcher. Courtesy Burton and Patricia Fletcher.

. . . by these interweaving patterns."[11] Magnolia and jac-aranda trees, for example, dominated the front of the east entrance to Bullock's Santa Ana and made singular and mul-tiple appearances throughout the landscape plan. Along the street, Queensland pittosporum intermingled with quartets of olive trees, which were set at each pedestrian entrance. A double allée of olive trees continued from the entrance in a consistent green visual line to the central mall, while a row of single-trunk Brazilian pepper trees, with one large jacaranda "drifted" in, carried the line southward along the east wall of the Bullock's store, and she continued the line to the southern edge of the property with a row of multi-trunk pepper trees.[12]

During the planning phase, Shellhorn salvaged existing trees whenever possible. The west end of the Santa Ana mall featured a twin-trunk Washington palm that she rescued and planted with a single palm to form a trio. When it became necessary to move a set of matching magnolia trees from Bullock's Pasadena to make way for a new parking structure in 1956, she boxed and stored them for later placement around the northeast corner of the Santa Ana store. Bullock's maintained those trees for almost two years, along with two large ficus and Senegal date and sago palms, until construction permitted replanting.[13]

Later, when the property for Bullock's Fashion Square in Sherman Oaks was purchased from a charity-run boarding school in 1960, there were at least twenty trees of significant size or character on the property that merited rescue. Two in particular caught her attention: an ancient Brazilian pepper tree twisted around an old steam vent and a magnificent old melaleuca whose branches were entangled in a rusted chain-link fence. Shellhorn extricated and precisely pruned the pepper to bring out its contorted branching structure—a fresh glance back at the ancient art of bonsai. The tree became the focal point of a sensational composition at the store entrance. She had the melaleuca carefully clipped free to serve as a substantial focal feature at the east end of the mall. The presence of each of these trees generated ideas for blending and repeating plantings throughout the site. The lance-shaped leaves of the melaleuca, for example, sparked the idea of using flaming red bottlebrush standards with similarly shaped leaves to delineate the western automobile entrance. Additional pepper trees were added to the plantings, "drifting" along the southern edge of the Bullock's building and blending with carob trees in the south parking lot.

Shellhorn accepted the troublesome nature of parking areas, viewing them as an essential part of a shopping center. In terms of square footage, they made up the largest portion of the project, and she was certain they could be as pleasing as the rest of the site.[14] The idea of treating a park-

Central mall with lawn, Fashion Square Santa Ana, 1977. Photograph by Ruth Shellhorn. Courtesy RSP.

'Nevadillo' olive trees in planters, Fashion Square Santa Ana, 1959. Photograph by Ruth Shellhorn. Courtesy RSP.

ing area as an oasis was unusual and with any other client might not have met with corporate approval, especially if the design decreased the number of potential parking spaces. But Shellhorn's conception of the shopping process as a total experience was fully embraced by Bullock's management. She often sketched diagrams for alternative vehicular access points even before architectural plans were undertaken, believing that this type of participation early in the design process improved the quality of finished projects.

As with all of her Fashion Squares, Shellhorn's exterior landscape design for the Santa Ana shopping center relied on

North entrance, Fashion Square Santa Ana, 1967. In the author's possession.

the subtle weaving and overlapping of seasonal flower color, leaf color, and leaf texture. This meant that color ebbed and flowed in different portions of the property depending on the time of the year. She wrote that she did not like "to use color in great masses, just for a splashy effect," adding: "Color, I feel, should be used to concentrate interest in an area, yet there must be gradual transition to the next area. I like to think of it as a wave of movement, stilled, but carrying from point to point, changing as the eye travels." At Santa Ana, magnolia trees, backed by red-berried Brazilian pepper trees, formed a transition to reddish-orange-flowering coral trees, espaliered red hibiscus and weeping red bottlebrush, with red-tipped sedum and tam juniper along the southern side of the building. The yellow flowers of Chinese flame tree and the groundcover of Aaron's beard intermingled with the coral hues of shrimp plant at the southern edge of the development. The "hot" color theme then "drifted" into dark pinks with the fluffy balls of pink powder puff, which were closely related in leaf texture and flower color to the silk tree. This tree's lighter pink blooms blended into the

Entrance drive, Fashion Square La Habra, 1972. Photograph by Dominick Culotta. In the author's possession.

Parking area entrance to Buffums', Fashion Square La Habra, 1972. Photograph by Dominick Culotta. In the author's possession.

grouping of magnolias, pink-flowering Indian hawthorn, Cape chestnut, and the rosy flower clusters of eucalyptus in the western parking area.[15]

Shellhorn occasionally eschewed color altogether, designing broad, luxuriant planting beds to buffer the sidewalk between parking areas and shops. These included groupings of plants that relied on harmonizing shades of green, the textural interest of leaves, and the shapes of the plants themselves. In the northern parking lot at Santa Ana she planted Hollywood juniper with jade plant and Hahn's ivy. On the western wall of Bullock's, she added yellow-green xylosma and a spot of color in a wall espalier of yellow- and white-flowering honeysuckle. The cumulative effect of these elements was more that of greenbelt than parking lot. Decades after these designs were installed, landscape architects spoke of Shellhorn's "stunning" and "elegant" effects.[16]

Planting compositions for all of the Bullock's pedestrian areas relied on bold forms, fine textures, and glossy leaves, but the designs were not repetitive. Completed eleven years after Bullock's Pasadena, Fashion Square Santa Ana amply demonstrated Shellhorn's maturing horticultural vocabulary. Here, she combined frequently used favorites—lemon-scented gum, giant bird-of-paradise, and Senegal date palm—in a background planter to soften the heft of a bulky building, but her compositions now included the finer groundcover textures of ornamental strawberry and sections of lawn, then a new concept in outdoor shopping center design.[17] In one foreground planter, she composed a setting with king palm and a variety of agaves, aloes, and succulents. This scene attracted pedestrian interest not only because of its burst of blooming plants but for its subtle variety, foliage patterns, and colors.

For the same reason, Shellhorn also specified trees with finely patterned leaves, detailed branch structures, or interesting bark texture to be placed near walkways. The gray-green tone of common olive trees, for example, did not suit Shellhorn's verdant parkway theme for Santa Ana, but she found their smaller leaves and craggy trunks so appealing that she tracked down a greener 'Nevadillo' variety.[18] Each tree, individually selected from a grove for its intended location, was positioned near a carefully chosen bench with a canopy

Planted buffers between sidewalk and parking area, Fashion Square La Habra, 1972. Photograph by Dominick Culotta. In the author's possession.

of shade, or an appropriate walkway with an overhanging branch.

The main pedestrian hub within the Santa Ana shopping center featured a rectangular pool, which Shellhorn surrounded with an intricate display of durable, low-growing succulents and cycad palms. The area served a dual purpose: in its early days, Bullock's management held informal fashion shows outdoors, and a temporary platform was constructed to cover the pool and plants so that models could sashay across the "stage"; Shellhorn even worked out a seating plan for the layout of chairs for the audience. When the shows were over, chairs and cover disappeared, and the pool and planting design with agaves in the foreground and a groundcover of aeonium and sedum became visible once again.[19]

One of Shellhorn's most sophisticated planting arrange-

Central mall, Fashion Square La Habra, 1972. Photograph by Dominick Culotta. In the author's possession.

ments at Santa Ana highlighted the store's north entrance. The scene was composed like a classical painting and balanced a hierarchical arrangement of elements, beginning with a lacy Japanese maple tree, a delicately shaped strawberry guava tree, and underplantings of a variety of ferns and Serbian bellflower. This welcoming arrangement of plants filtered the view of the entrance doors, adding a sense of elegance. Erik Katzmaier, an Orange County landscape architect, recalled that Shellhorn's composition was the first time he had seen strawberry guava, with its fine branching character and reddish, peeling bark, in such a setting. Shoppers loved the area and clamored to re-create the plantings in their home gardens.[20]

By the end of the 1960s, Shellhorn's Fashion Square designs had emerged as a recognizable style sought after by landscape and garden enthusiasts throughout Southern California. She frequently answered letters from shoppers who wanted advice about how to achieve the "Southern California look" in their own gardens. After the Fashion Square at La Habra opened in 1968, *Sunset Magazine* published a six-page article showing homeowners how to re-create Shellhorn's "handsomely designed, lavishly executed, and carefully maintained" landscapes.[21] Detailed information was included about espaliers, small spaces, planting combinations, climate control, and screening for views. Potted and hanging plants played a significant role in the *Sunset* article, which showed how Shellhorn clustered pots and filled them with rounded, drooping, or arching forms, such as jade, asparagus, or sago palm, to mark transition spaces. Smaller pots were hung above eye level to add interest and "atmosphere." Larger pots were filled with espaliers to soften stark, unrelieved expanses of wall, including large-leafed evergreen grape or compositions of agave and juniper.[22]

The article did not discuss the contribution made by

Harry Kueser, Shellhorn's husband and business partner, who was also a skilled carpenter and handyman. Kueser devised the elaborate espalier patterns and contrived the various hook-and-wire installations that made her delightful displays work. A picture hook and wire guided tiny, twining Guinea gold vine on thinly plastered walls, wire threaded through sturdy eye bolts supported thick-stalked bougainvillea and cup-of-gold, and splayed wires and ties trained

Central fountain, Fashion Square La Habra, 1972. Photograph by Dominick Culotta. In the author's possession.

brilliant hibiscus, while cat's claw climbed and spread its exuberant patterns with no help at all. *Sunset* suggested that these forms could be studied as "the ancient art of espalier," but they were obviously a more modern, freely interpreted expression of that art.

In 1966 in Washington, D.C., Lady Bird Johnson presented Shellhorn with the American Association of Nurserymen's National Industrial Landscaping Award, one of

Entrance to Buffums', Fashion Square La Habra, 1972. Photograph by Dominick Culotta. In the author's possession.

Shellhorn's many honors for Bullock's Fashion Square Santa Ana.[23] Although it is difficult to measure the professional impact of Shellhorn's Fashion Square landscape designs, the public treated them like parks. Even when stores were closed, people came to walk around, have picnics on the lawn, take wedding photographs, and paint.[24]

Virtually all of Shellhorn's outdoor landscape design for Santa Ana was destroyed by the addition of a new indoor shopping structure in the late 1980s. The property now operates under new ownership as Westfield MainPlace. Remnants of Shellhorn's plantings are still visible in areas around Macy's (the remodeled Bullock's structure) and along the front and side perimeters of the property. The open-air Sherman Oaks shopping center was fully enclosed in the late 1980s, closing off three entry courts to make room for more retail stores, and additional parking structures were added on the southern edge of the property. The center became Westfield Fashion Square in 2005. Bullock's Fashion Square Del Amo was the subject of an extensive remodel in the 1990s and now operates as the Del Amo Fashion Center. All the surface parking lots, with the exception of the west area, have been covered by an enclosed shopping structure and multilevel parking. The patio courtyard is still in place, as are some perimeter plantings along Hawthorne Boulevard. After a long period of economic decline, the La Habra Fashion Square was demolished in stages between 1990 and 1995. It was replaced with an enclosed development, the La Habra Marketplace, in 1996. More than sixty mature trees were removed during construction, and none of Shellhorn's original landscape design remains.

MARLBOROUGH SCHOOL

LOS ANGELES, CALIFORNIA

1966–1984

The commission to design a new landscape plan for the Marlborough School, a private college preparatory school for girls, came to Shellhorn because of her particular interest in trees. In the 1960s the school hired the noted architectural firm William L. Pereira & Associates to redesign the campus in a modern style with respect for its Colonial Revival architectural tradition dating back to 1916. Although pleased with Pereira's work, the school had lost confidence in its landscape architect.[1] While shopping in a local nursery, one of the school's trustees, Charles Munger, noticed that all the best trees were tagged and on hold for Ruth Shellhorn. He told his wife, Nancy, an alumna of the school and a member of the building committee, and Shellhorn was promptly hired as executive landscape architect. This project was the first of her many residential, campus, and park design commissions for the Mungers and their friends.

Shellhorn's first landscape design, completed in 1967,

took into account the context of the walled school—a leafy residential neighborhood of early twentieth-century mansions known as Hancock Park. Elm and magnolia trees bordered the four-acre site on the corner of Third Street and Rossmore Avenue. Because Pereira's two-story modernist library was most visible at the street intersection, Shellhorn anchored one corner of the building with a pair of Canary

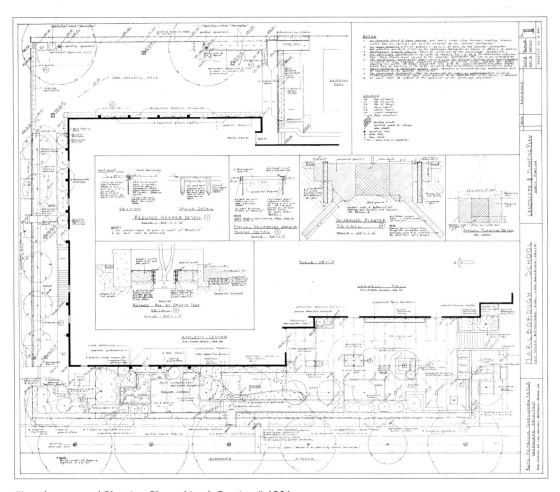

"Landscape and Planting Plan—North Portion," 1981. Courtesy RSP.

Library atrium, c. 1980. Courtesy Marlborough School.

Island pine trees and created a buffer of additional magnolia trees and white-flowering evergreen pear trees along the perimeter of the property. She also developed a botanical "signature" for the campus—espaliered pear trees repeated along the perimeter wall with a groundcover of star jasmine. This green and white theme was emphasized with hedges of viburnum and xylosma, large accent specimens of Hollywood juniper shrub masses, and additional groundcover of Hahn's ivy.

In her landscape plan for the campus, Shellhorn focused on carving usable outdoor living areas from the available space. Two broad panels of open lawn flanked either side of the front entrance to the school. A pair of two-story buildings with offices and classrooms extending north from the library featured covered walkways and balconies supported by columns, which Shellhorn wrapped in lavender wisteria, violet trumpet vine, and mauve royal trumpet vine to honor the school colors, purple and white. A passageway between the buildings led to the back lawn and a prominent fountain with wraparound seating. Since this gathering place was shaded and subject to heavy traffic, Shellhorn planted a durable palette of xylosma shrubs and foreground plantings of cast-iron plant, aralia, and giant lily turf. These were combined with the black leaves and violet flowers of carpet bugle groundcover and yellow day-lilies, which added contrast to the all-green composition and complemented the purple flowers sprinkled throughout the campus.

An atrium was constructed in the center of the library, and Shellhorn carried the outdoor courtyard theme to this interior space with a gridded paving plan, similar to the exterior paving, and included benches arranged to facilitate conversational groups. She used a selection of plants that fared well in low light. These included a gradation of leaf textures and shapes that ranged from Japanese aralia, with its wide palmate leaves, and strap-leafed clivia hybrids to spiky-leafed mahonia shrubs to heavenly bamboo, an assortment of ferns, and giant lily turf groundcover. The composition also preserved an existing group of eugenia trees, a decision that required Shellhorn to design special tree wells.[2]

Shellhorn's focus on exploring opportunities for outdoor living continued in her 1981 plan for an expansion of the

Jacaranda trees adjacent to classroom building, c. 1987. Courtesy Marlborough School.

Rear lawn with fountain, 1980. Courtesy Marlborough School.

school, in which she linked the existing library, classrooms, offices, and a new gymnasium with a string of modernist-inspired outdoor rooms that also honored the school's traditional architectural roots. She balanced asymmetrical garden and structural elements with a pleasing variety of interconnected walkways, semi-enclosed courtyards that kept the scale of the spaces small, and abundant seating areas. Water features and subtropical plantings contributed to this relaxed atmosphere. Deciduous shade trees—jacaranda, silk tree, liquidambar, ginkgo, and purple orchid tree—allowed winter

North view toward gymnasium, 1987. Photograph by Ruth Shellhorn. Courtesy RSP.

sun into these areas and made them practical for use virtually year-round.[3]

Along the western side of the school, Shellhorn wove together a series of overlapping garden areas on a north–south axis and connected them with concrete paving and a variable brick grid that shrank and expanded as it moved from one garden to the next. This procession began at the flag court at the front of the school, an area of about fifty square feet bordered by a brick wall with built-in wood slat benches on two sides. A large pear tree in the center cast afternoon shade from the southwest sun on the benches, and an existing fern

Crane sculpture fountain, 1987. Photograph by Robert M. Fletcher. Courtesy Burton and Patricia Fletcher. In the author's possession.

pine marked the steps up into the donors' garden, which served as another entrance into the school.[4] The donors' garden featured a single pear tree shading built-in concrete benches and a small reflecting pool. This area bordered an entrance into the gymnasium, lined by orchid and jacaranda trees, and the high wall of Caswell Hall auditorium to the right, which was softened with the tracery of espaliered ornamental pear and lavender starflower.

In Shellhorn's 1967 plan, two rectangles of lawn separated the old gymnasium from a perimeter wall along the street. One lawn section was replaced with a fountain pool in 1982 to accommodate a bronze sculpture of cranes.[5] Shellhorn designed a brick pond, filled with water lilies and equisetum, to display the birds in an aquatic habitat. A walkway continued north from the fountain to the senior garden, which was completely enclosed with high hedges and a deciduous canopy of pink-flowering silk floss tree. The center of the garden was paved with the same concrete and brick as the rest of the gardens but included an array of stepping stones etched with each senior class's year of graduation. School colors popped out in foreground plantings of purple-flowering hebe and blue agapanthus.[6]

Shellhorn's landscape design secured a Los Angeles Beautiful award for the Marlborough School in 1973. After acquiring an adjacent two acres of land for athletic fields, the school underwent another major expansion in 2006. The library was demolished and rebuilt, and the interior atrium was replaced with an open-corridor atrium. Land Images, a local design firm, renovated the landscape design, but the series of garden spaces designed by Shellhorn along the western edge of the school remains essentially intact.

Front entrance, 2012. Photograph by Kevin Johnson.

HIXON GARDEN

PASADENA, CALIFORNIA

1975–1990

In 1971 the architect A. Quincy Jones, best known for his modernist designs, was hired to remodel a residence on the eastern side of a quiet cul-de-sac on a hilltop in Pasadena. The homeowners, Alexander and Adelaide Hixon, subsequently acquired the house across the street and kept their former home for use as a guesthouse.[1] Jones returned to implement a substantial remodel of this second home in 1975. His modern residence featured soaring ceilings, a lath-roofed patio, and sweeping views across the south-facing slope. The Hixons, who knew many of Shellhorn's satisfied clients, hired her to design a landscape that would unify their two properties.[2]

Shellhorn created a dramatic backdrop for the owners' collection of sculptural art, which reflected time spent in Africa and the South Pacific, by carefully selecting daring compositions of succulents, subtropical plants, and hardscape materials. Boulders, river rocks, and gravel were used

Flame tree at front entrance, 2012. Photograph by Kevin Johnson.

throughout the landscape to evoke the aquatic culture of the Pacific Islands. In spite of the hilly topography, Shellhorn developed a landscape design of informal curving walkways, rounded planting beds, interconnecting stairways, and asymmetrically framed views to link the two homes and the space in between. She took full advantage of the fact that every room in Jones's structure included both physical and visual access to the out-of-doors. The result of their shared vision merged outdoor and indoor to make a dramatic connection between landscape and architecture.

An access road to both properties wound uphill and terminated in the cul-de-sac, which functioned as a private circular motor court. An existing peppermint tree stood in a large concrete planter that seemed to float over a pond of river rock. Shellhorn supplemented existing Aleppo pine and deodar cedar trees, deciduous flowering peach trees, and a mock orange hedge on the east side of the motor court drive

Hillside planting, 1978. Photograph by Ruth Shellhorn. Courtesy RSP.

with a swath of white-flowering plants, including multi-trunk evergreen pear trees, and Chinese magnolia, shrubs of Indian hawthorn and Sandankwa viburnum, and ground-covers of Algerian ivy and white vinca. The composition of deciduous and evergreen textures in combination with a

Entrance to breakfast patio, 1979. Photograph by Ruth Shellhorn. Courtesy RSP.

disciplined all-white flowering palette created an exotic yet restful effect. These plantings enclosed a small formal garden with a rectangular pool, whose interior Shellhorn painted black. At the owners' request, she added a water-chilling system to support cold-water trout.[3] She bordered the pool

Fountain, 1979. Photograph by Ruth Shellhorn. Courtesy RSP.

Lava rock wall, 1979. Photograph by Ruth Shellhorn. Courtesy RSP.

with blue fescue, placed foxtail agave against a row of Italian cypress along the back wall, and added two enormous white-flowering azaleas to the foreground, creating a serene space for showcasing two of the owners' favorite sculptures.

Along the west side of the drive Shellhorn chose a drift

Lawn and lava wall, 1979. Photograph by Ruth Shellhorn. Courtesy RSP.

of three Canary Island pine trees and a group of tam junipers to balance the conifers on the east. This evergreen planting terminated with the placement of a beautifully twisted Japanese black pine clustered with bird-of-paradise, juniper, and potentilla to screen a utility wall. As the houses came into

Interconnecting planter between living room and garden, 1979. Photograph by author.

full view, motorists drove under the pool of shade cast by a Chinese flame tree and entered the motor court with distant views to the south. Four white oleander trees, trained as standards and spaced about twenty feet apart at the southern edge of the court, framed the expansive view. The scheme was a simple but remarkably effective means of tying together the two residences.

Although the property sloped steeply downward beyond the white oleander scrim, Shellhorn claimed enough space to connect the properties with a walkway of railroad-tie steps adjacent to a riotous display of low-maintenance succulents anchored by retaining walls of dry-stacked broken concrete. Aeonium, agave, aloe, and chartreuse euphorbia tumbled across the slopes and nestled under native toyon. To the natural rock outcroppings, Shellhorn added a border of prostrate ceanothus, Pride of Madeira, and a prized specimen Canary Island dragon tree. She used a number of native plants in these compositions, but it was not her intent to replicate the native landscape. Rather, she introduced vivid botanical forms that linked the architectural and artistic drama of the house, gardens, and sculpture with the native landscape.

The entrance path to the new residence was paved in polished black granite panels that shimmered like still water. Shellhorn carried the effect of water into the entrance patio, which she paved with varying sizes of aggregate stepping stones embedded in a stream of Rosarita river rock and black pebbles. This path led to a more stable surface of concrete rectangles surrounded by black river rocks and a paved circle for dining sheltered by a multi-trunk strawberry tree. Rangpur lime, feathery rhaphis palm, white wisteria, and agapanthus enhanced the tropical effect.[4]

On the left side of the entry Shellhorn created a small

patio with potted citrus trees and a seating area suggesting a rock outcropping.[5] Below the patio, a decomposed granite and railroad-tie pathway was laid out to take advantage of the south view and then turned right into a modernist grotto paved in stepping stones, river rock, and gravel. Water poured down from a steel spout more than eight feet above into a blue-tiled fountain. Blooming succulents on a lava rock wall, aloes, and bird-of-paradise added to the drama of the scene.

Lockwood de Forest Jr. had long incorporated succulents in his work, a subject of interest to Shellhorn, who was always in search of low-maintenance plants with unusual shapes and textures. Early in her career she visited specialty nurseries with de Forest and accumulated a small collection of books, including J. R. Brown's *Succulents for the Amateur* (1939) and *Unusual Plants: 110 Spectacular Photographs of Succulents* (1954), both published in Pasadena by the Abbey Garden Press. The Hixon garden illustrates the success of Shellhorn's experiments with succulents and her ability to create a dramatic composition with the plants she deemed appropriate to each setting.

Below the living room window Shellhorn created an area of lawn, which contributed a vital space in the composition. West of the lawn, a seating area provided a transition to a stairway constructed of railroad-tie risers with treads of two-inch Mexican river rock pounded on edge. The stair treatment recalled a cobbled path that Shellhorn had seen in Amapala, Honduras, during her travels in Central America.[6] The stairway led to the guesthouse, curving in an arc around a specimen giant bird-of-paradise, which she had placed by crane at great expense. The twenty-five-foot tree anchored the curve of the stairway and shaded the living room. At the top of the stairway, an elegant pitched-roof lath structure formed a shaded patio between a small guesthouse and the living room with large specimens of sago palm clumps, azalea, and staghorn fern. A winding decomposed granite path studded with boulders and scattered ribbons of gravel led to the back of the house.

Stairway, 1977. Photograph by Ruth Shellhorn. Courtesy RSP.

In the Hixon garden, Shellhorn was able to cater to her client's artistic sensibilities and, by relating her design to its modernist setting, create a timeless quality. She continued to work with the homeowners and prepare regular maintenance reports until her retirement in 1990. The original owner was maintaining the garden in 2015.

BRACKENRIDGE / NIVEN GARDEN

SOUTH PASADENA, CALIFORNIA

1978–1990

During the 1970s, Shellhorn received an increasing number of residential commissions, many from the network of influential Los Angeles women who had come to favor her. In 1978 three of Shellhorn's clients, Ann Mudd, Adelaide Hixon, and Ernestine Avery, recommended her to their friend Maria Antonia (Tony) Brackenridge. Shellhorn was hired to develop a new landscape design for the house Brackenridge's parents had purchased in 1943 and where she had lived since childhood.[1]

Located on a quiet cul-de-sac in the estate area of South Pasadena, the two-story house and garden was sited on a level area, with a generous setback that gently sloped downward toward the street. The noted architect Garrett Beekman Van Pelt designed the Monterey Colonial home in 1929. With its front-facing overhanging balcony, deep porch and patio, and abundant windows, the house offered numerous opportunities to interact with the landscape.[2]

In 1978 Shellhorn found the front garden plantings neglected and overgrown. From the street, a set of steep steps led up a narrow formal walkway to the front entrance. The front balcony was obscured from view by a line of two large alder trees. Shellhorn wanted a landscape design that would acknowledge the intent of Van Pelt's architecture and take better advantage of the potential for outdoor living. Her new landscape design reconfigured access from the street to create a more gracious entrance by offsetting the axis of the walkway, widening it to six feet, and paving it in red brick. Breaking the formal axis of the path reduced the steepness of the steps at the street and allowed for an easier arrival process.

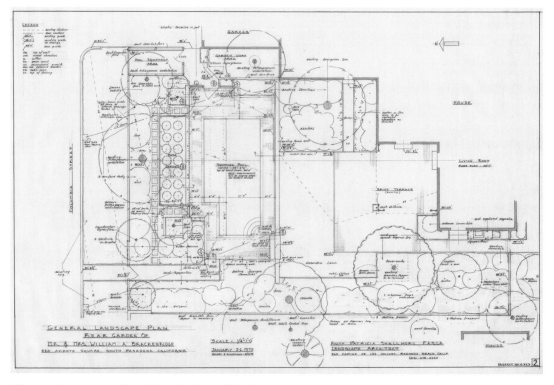

"General Landscape Plan, Rear Garden of Mr. & Mrs. William A. Brackenridge," 1979. Courtesy RSP.

Balcony entwined with jasmine, 1987. Photograph by Robert M. Fletcher. Courtesy Burton and Patricia Fletcher.

Front garden path of decomposed granite, 1987. Photograph by Robert M. Fletcher.
Courtesy Burton and Patricia Fletcher.

Rear garden, 2006. Photograph by Ron Stinnett.

Shellhorn freely experimented with combinations of plants for the front garden that offered a variety of textures and patterns. Her simple massing of flora introduced a casual formality that gave this garden its distinctive regional character. She reshaped the existing alder trees to filter the view from the street while allowing a glimpse of the fine details of the balcony. A magnolia, trained as an espalier, spread across one side of the house. Purple-flowering lavender starflower was also espaliered and kept thin so that it cast shadows against the wall. Star jasmine grew as a vine along the balcony and, in the foreground, anchored the composition

Patio, 2006. Photograph by Ron Stinnett.

as a groundcover. Shellhorn used color carefully; the white flowers on the magnolia and evergreen pear trees and white blossoms on the star jasmine groundcover added elegance to a simple planting plan. A broad path of decomposed granite between the driveway and the front porch, a treatment Shellhorn frequently used in her residential work, suggests her effort to conserve water.[3]

Tony's daughter remembers the backyard during the years before Shellhorn began her work as "lots of little box hedges and a mishmash of citrus and a vegetable garden."[4] In redesigning the back garden to accommodate a new swimming pool, Shellhorn was most concerned about retaining a

Swimming pool, seating wall, garden, and patio, 2006. Photograph by Ron Stinnett.

scale appropriate to the space and preventing the turquoise water of the pool from becoming a visual distraction. She solved both problems by sculpting a lower grade for the pool at the far back of the property and retaining a low intervening brick wall that screened the pool from the patio. Along with the lawn separating the patio from the pool, this arrangement added another layer of depth to the garden. The eighteen-inch-high wall also provided several yards of impromptu seating.

Although the back garden featured a more complex pattern of texture and variety than the front, the consistent use of white-flowering plants provided visual coherence. Larger background shrubs included 'Snow White' Indian hawthorn and viburnum, which displayed fluffy white clusters of flowers; cocculus, ilex, and variegated pittosporum created a spectrum of dark to light greens. A large weeping elm, a eucalyptus, and a deciduous liquidambar tree with fiery fall color enriched this tapestry of foliage. After incorporating into her plan an existing jacaranda tree, a scattering of pink- and magenta-flowering camellias and azaleas, and a wisteria vine twining along the eaves of the back patio, Shellhorn emphasized this color palette by adding espaliered lavender starflower and pink powder puff, with shocking-pink blooms on the garden wall just east of the kitchen. Among the plantings around the pool were citrus trees and gardenia shrubs, ivy vines along the fence, grape ivy and mondo grass groundcovers, and a purple-leaf plum tree. A towering avocado tree completed the design.[5]

In 1980 Tony married her second husband, Robert Forbes Niven, and, as a wedding gift, commissioned Shellhorn to design rose gardens for him on the east and west edges of the front garden. Every year until 1987, Shellhorn returned to this garden and prepared reports on its condition, helping Tony learn how to tend and refine the plantings. Through her passion for plants, Shellhorn instilled a similar desire in many of her clients to maintain and improve their gardens. In a letter, Tony Niven thanked her for "the gift of my beautiful garden," calling her "a very superior lady who has helped and taught me a lot—and whom I am proud to have as a friend."[6] The Niven garden was kept in meticulous condition until the owner's death in 2006 and remains well maintained today.

DOERR GARDEN

PASADENA, CALIFORNIA

1978–1992

In 1950, Shellhorn acquired one of Florence Yoch's former clients and began a long-term effort to preserve her gardens.[1] Yoch's period revival gardens were elegant, concise adaptations of European prototypes that often juxtaposed traditional design elements with natural features. In the 1930s and 1940s she was particularly concerned with designing low-maintenance gardens, a passion Shellhorn shared. As she took on the stewardship of Yoch's gardens, Shellhorn endeavored to respect their original designs, and the most noteworthy of Shellhorn's efforts, the Doerr garden in Pasadena, lives on thanks to her meticulous supervision following Yoch's death in 1972.

Originally designed for Ira L. Bryner, a successful oilman, in 1928, the garden was part of a property that spread across three lots and sloped steeply down to the street. Yoch collaborated closely with the architect, Roland Coate, who positioned the residence with views of the San Gabriel Mountains to the north and the nearby Arroyo to the west.[2]

Pond, 1985. Photograph by Robert M. Fletcher. Courtesy Burton and Patricia Fletcher.

The garden was actually three gardens, each reflecting inspiration from a different European precedent. On the terrace closest to the house was a small citrus grove of orange, lime, and tangerine trees reminiscent of simple Spanish gardens; the second terrace displayed roses in a formal elongated oval, a reference to French gardens; and the bottom terrace presented a broad panel of lawn alluding to English garden traditions. Eleven flights of stairs connected the terraces, offering "delicate calibrations of level" similar to the water parterre at the Villa Gamberaia in Florence.[3]

In 1941, Albert and Harriet Doerr purchased the property and hired Yoch to return and simplify maintenance of

Lower lawn and pond, 1987. Photograph by Robert M. Fletcher. Courtesy Burton and Patricia Fletcher.

the garden in response to a decrease in staff. Yoch suggested replacing a tulip bed with a paved area and prepared a nineteen-page manual of instructions for the subsequent care of the garden.[4] Both Florence Yoch and Albert Doerr died in 1972. Six years later, Harriet consulted Shellhorn about the possibility of either selling off the garden portion of the property or altering it to make it easier to manage.[5] Shellhorn advised preserving the garden.

Shellhorn maintained the garden's original structure, preparing no formal landscape plans but visiting Doerr's garden several times a year to supervise hardscape repairs and address small changes. Her files reveal careful research and experimentation with newly available plants, as well as a capacity to adapt to new materials when formerly available brick, stone, and gravel sources disappeared. Shellhorn restrained herself from making an imprint on this garden, and in doing so she not only preserved it but also maintained the

Porch in winter, 1987. Photograph by Robert M. Fletcher. Courtesy Burton and Patricia Fletcher.

Citrus trees, 1987. Photograph by Robert M. Fletcher. Courtesy Burton and Patricia Fletcher.

intent of the original design. In 1988 she wrote to Yoch's biographer: "Florence was one of a kind. The fact that so many of her gardens are being lovingly cared for to preserve her designs is a real tribute. I had lunch with Harriett Doerr last Tuesday and I went over the garden with her making suggestions. I have tried, in my recommendations[,] to preserve the spirit of the garden Florence created."[6]

The small changes Shellhorn did make helped lend cohesion to the garden. During the late 1970s she substituted high-maintenance perennials surrounding the lawn and rose garden with bushy, frequently blooming Fielder's White and Alaska azaleas. These sun-tolerant hybrids proved a judicious choice when an attack of oak root fungus began to claim the garden's major shade providers.[7] As the oak trees succumbed, they were supplanted with deciduous trees resistant to the fungus, such as jacaranda, liquidambar, and evergreen pear. Chinese holly replaced viburnum hedges and orange jessa-

Rose garden in winter, 1987. Photograph by Robert M. Fletcher. Courtesy Burton and Patricia Fletcher.

mine replaced toyon. Shellhorn managed to retain Yoch's subtle textural effects, and the white line of azaleas strengthened the axial relationship between the pool and the pond.

As the years passed, Shellhorn's continued maintenance of the garden led to additional adaptations and alterations. In preparation for a garden club tour in the spring of 1980, she found herself searching for rock cinder mulch to match the existing gravel around the rose island, placed fifty years earlier. 'Transcendent' and floribunda crab apples were planted in the upper terrace, and the dichondra lawn was resodded and later replaced with turf. In the late 1980s, when neighbors installed a swimming pool, Shellhorn planted a bank of puka,

Path between upper and middle gardens, 1987. Photograph by Kevin Johnson.

Garden from porch, 2012. Photograph by Kevin Johnson.

a screening shrub with dark, leathery leaves. A square patch of lawn was paved over to make way for more patio space and, in the early 1990s, she redesigned the little garden by the house, adding a birdbath in the center of a brick court.[8]

In 1996, almost twenty years after Shellhorn began her work, Harriet Doerr wrote a lyrical essay about her love for this garden and the bittersweet memories time and change evoked.[9] Shellhorn's preservation of the Doerr garden was a fitting tribute from a student who owed much of her success to the inspiration of her mentor; she took pride in carrying out Yoch's lessons of meticulous maintenance, preserving a legacy that is now shared.

Garden house in lower garden, 2012. Photograph by Kevin Johnson.

Porch structure covered with wisteria, 2005. Photograph by Robert M. Fletcher. Courtesy Burton and Patricia Fletcher.

NOTES

ABBREVIATIONS

RSP   Ruth Patricia Shellhorn Papers (Collection 1757),
             UCLA Library Special Collections, Charles E. Young
             Research Library, UCLA

Shellhorn diaries   Diaries, 1926–2006, boxes 351, 355–60, RSP

OVERVIEW

1. Doug Stapleton, the editor of *Landscape Design and Construction,* described it in an unsigned article as "the California scene"; "A Study of Ruth Patricia Shellhorn, Award Winning Landscape Architect," October 1967, 7. Shellhorn herself later recalled that the first president of Bullock's wanted "a California look"; Pasadena Heritage Oral History Project, "Interview with Ruth Patricia Shellhorn," conducted by Molly Johnson (Pasadena: Pasadena Oral History Project, 2002), 34–35. More recently, Kevin Starr has identified the style as "the California style or the Quality California look," in *Golden Dreams: California in an Age of Abundance, 1950–1963* (New York: Oxford University Press, 2009), 35. A Fashion Square Santa Ana press release referred to "the feeling of early California"; "Fashion Square Landscape Plan Creates Garden-like Effect," September 16, 1958. In "Shopping Ease Featured in Store's Design," the *Pasadena Star-News* (September 9, 1947) heralded the store as embodying "the spirit of Southern California itself." Shellhorn also later referred to the style as "the California Atmo-

sphere"; quoted in "Santa Ana Has Beautiful New Fashion Square," *Southwest Builder and Contractor,* August 22, 1958, 8.

2. David C. Streatfield, "New Dimensions in Landscape Architecture and Environmental Design," conference paper, University of California, Irvine, May 1, 1983, copy in the author's possession.

3. Shellhorn, Pasadena Oral History interview, 43; Sam Watters, email to author, February 28, 2012.

4. Ruth Shellhorn, interview by author, November 17, 2004.

5. Bullock's Fashion Square, Santa Ana, maintenance records, box 6, folder 1, RSP.

6. I am grateful to David C. Streatfield for sharing this observation.

7. Shellhorn, interviews by author, November 17 and December 6, 2004, and telephone interview by author, August 1, 2006.

8. Ruth Shellhorn to James J. Yoch, April 20, 1981, in the author's possession.

9. Shellhorn diaries, February 10, 1930.

10. Shellhorn, interview by author for The Cultural Landscape Foundation, February 3, 2005, 3–4, and interview by author, December 6, 2004; Shellhorn diaries, September 6, 1930.

11. Daniel Wayne Krall, "Visions of Outdoor Art: One Hundred Years of Landscape Architecture Education at Cornell," unpublished manuscript, 206, copy in the author's possession.

12. Shellhorn, KKG correspondence file, in the author's possession.

13. Krall, "Visions of Outdoor Art," 102–12.

14. Ibid., 250.

15. Among the lectures in the city and regional planning course was one by the Boston-based planning advocate Flavel Shurtleff, who spoke on New York City planning issues. Shellhorn diaries, March 14 and April 17, 1932.

16. Shellhorn diaries, March 12, 1932.

17. Fletcher Steele, "New Pioneering in Garden Design," *Landscape Architecture Quarterly* 20 (April 1930): 159–77. The *Contemporary American Sculpture* exhibition was held at the California Palace of the Legion of Honor in San Francisco in 1929.

18. Shellhorn, travel journal, June 21–July 2, 1933, in the author's possession; Shellhorn diaries, June 12, 1933.

19. David C. Streatfield, email to author, March 11, 2008.

20. Shellhorn, Pasadena Oral History interview, 37.

21. Yoch and Council also worked on Depression-era film sets, including such classics as *The Good Earth* (1937), *Gone with the Wind* (1939), and *How Green Was My Valley* (1941). See James J. Yoch, *Landscaping the American Dream: The Gardens and Film Sets of Florence Yoch, 1890–1972* (New York: Harry N. Abrams, 1989), 182–85.

22. Shellhorn, interview by author, March 20, 2006.

23. Victoria Padilla, *Southern California Gardens: An Illustrated History* (Berkeley: University of California Press, 1961), 117–18; Shellhorn, interviews by author, November 17, 2004, and January 25, 2006.

24. Esther McCoy, *Five California Architects* (Santa Monica: Hennessey and Ingalls, 2004), 107–9, 83–85.

25. Wallace Neff Jr., *Wallace Neff: Architect of California's Golden Age* (Santa Barbara: Capra Press, 1986); David Gebhard and Robert Winter, *An Architectural Guidebook to Los Angeles* (Layton, UT: Gibbs Smith, 2003), 380–449.

26. Shellhorn, interview by author, February 8, 2006. At Bashford's suggestion, Shellhorn inquired about Junior Associate membership at the end of 1933 and received a strong letter of recommendation from a Cornell University professor. Walter Ewald to Katherine Bashford, Pacific Coast Chapter, ASLA, November 24, 1933, in the author's possession.

27. Steven Keylon, "The California Landscapes of Katherine Bashford," *Eden: Journal of the California Garden & Landscape History Society* 16 (Fall 2013): 3.

28. Ann Scheid, "Beatrix Farrand in California," *Eden: Journal of the California Garden & Landscape History Society* 14 (Spring 2011): 1–13.

29. On this tradition see Louise A. Mozingo and Linda Jewell, eds., *Women in Landscape Architecture: Essays on History and Practice* (Jefferson, NC: McFarland, 2012); Thaisa Way, *Unbounded Practice: Women and Landscape Architecture in the Early Twentieth Century* (Charlottesville: University of Virginia Press, 2009); and Sonja Dümpelmann and John Beardsley, eds., *Women, Modernity, and Landscape Architecture* (Abingdon, UK: Routledge, 2015).

30. Marie Barnidge-McIntyre, "Ralph Dalton Cornell," in *Pioneers of American Landscape Design,* ed. Charles A. Birnbaum and Robin Karson (New York: McGraw-Hill, 2000), 70–72; Shellhorn diaries, February 5, 1934; Shellhorn, interview by author, November 3, 2004.

31. Ruth Shellhorn, "Mr. Cornell," *California Horticultural Journal* 33 (October 1972): 160–61; Shellhorn, interview by author, November 3, 2004.

32. "Will Display Many Designs," *Los Angeles Times,* September 16, 1934, 23; Steven Keylon and Barbara Lamprecht, emails to author, February 6, 2014.

33. Shellhorn's project index, 1935–1988, box 361, RSP.

34. According to her project index, Shellhorn completed landscape designs for Green's own residence in Glendale in 1935; two offices for Green, one in Los Angeles in 1936 and a second in Glendale in 1948; and a home/office design for Musselwhite in 1937.

35. Shellhorn diaries, February 28, 1936; Shellhorn's project index (filed under "O," for "Other").

36. Shellhorn diaries, July 1936, April 13, 1936, March 29, 1937, and May 22, 1937.

37. Shellhorn diaries, March 19, 1937.

38. *House and Garden,* September 1937, 25. Shellhorn was not given credit as the landscape architect.

39. Shellhorn diaries, November 1, 1937; "Improve Flower Shows," *Sunset Magazine,* April, 1938, 27.

40. Shellhorn diaries, August 1 and September 17, 1938. The garden design for L. H. and Evelyn Jenkins, with architect Arthur Hutchason, was completed in 1936; the exhibit board with plan and photographs is in the author's possession.

41. "Residence of Mr. and Mrs. Leslie H. Crocker, Whittier," and "Residence of Mr. and Mrs. Robert W. Meyers, Whittier," *Architect and Engineer,* September 1940, 30–31, both with William H. Harrison. Plans and photographs of a garden for Mr. and Mrs. John H. Howard (1935) were shown in the *House and Garden* "Architect's Competition" in 1937 and featured in *California Arts and Architecture,* April 1939, 26.

42. Shellhorn diaries, May 3, 1939, and September 9–15, 1948.

43. "One Generous Patio for Entertaining . . . Another Secluded Patio for Privacy," *Sunset Magazine,* July 1955, 62–63; "How Planting Can Soften the Rigid Lines of Garden Steps," June 1954, 70; "These Garden Steps Invite You to Pause . . . Enjoy the Plants Nearby," February 1956, 64–65; Shellhorn diaries, June 27, 1951.

44. These *Sunset* articles were "Do's and Don'ts in Garden Design," October 1939, 45; "If You Want Space for Games," November 1939, 44; "If You Want Space for Gardening," December 1939, 42; "Your Garden's Center of Interest," January 1940, 45; "Frame Your Garden Picture," February 1940, 47; "Balance in Garden Design," March 1940, 62; and "Scale and Proportion in Garden Design," April 1940, 64.

45. Shellhorn, "Do's and Don'ts in Garden Design."

46. Cornell had been pressing Shellhorn to begin preparing her required portfolio as early as April 1939. Shellhorn diaries, April 28, 1939. The portfolio is in the author's possession. Tommy Tomson, a self-taught landscape architect, designed the settings for Los Angeles's Union Station and the Santa Anita Racetrack during the 1930s, and later founded and completed a master plan for the city of Palm Desert. Steven Keylon, unpublished manuscript, copy in the author's possession.

47. Shellhorn diaries, September 5, 1931, and January 20, 1936, and interviews by author, November 3 and 29, 2004.

48. Shellhorn, interview by author, November 17, 2004; Steven Keylon, emails to author, February 6 and May 5, 2014.

49. Shellhorn diaries, September 1942.

50. Shellhorn diaries, September 6, 1944.

51. Shellhorn diaries, October 8 and December 19, 1944.

52. Shellhorn, interview by author, November 3, 2004.

53. Shellhorn's ASLA files and her "Open Letter to California Landscape Architects," February 25, 1946, both in the author's possession. When licensure was finally established in 1954, practicing landscape architects were "grandfathered in," and Shellhorn was issued license no. 322 on June 25, 1954.

54. Shellhorn's meeting notes, August 24 and September 28, 1946, in the author's possession.

55. Shellhorn's meeting notes, March 29 and May 4, 1946, May 1947, and June 29, 1946, in the author's possession.

56. Lockwood de Forest Jr. to Shellhorn, April 30, 1948, box 373, folder 4, RSP.

57. "A Study of Ruth Patricia Shellhorn, Award Winning Landscape Architect," *Landscape Design and Construction* 13 (October 1967): 5.

58. Ruth Shellhorn, "Thoughts on Landscape Architecture," unpublished essay, 1961, 4, in the author's possession.

59. Shellhorn, interview by author, November 3, 2004. When the Westwood structure was remodeled in 1956, Bullock's management gave her the job and turned over to her the maintenance supervision.

60. Shellhorn, interview by author, November 29, 2004.

61. Louis Naidorf, interviews by author, February 2007.

62. Quoted in Robert Cahn, "The Man Who Changes Skylines," *Saturday Evening Post,* November 22, 1958, 33.

63. Shellhorn, "Thoughts on Landscape Architecture," 4.

64. Shellhorn to Glenn Rick, Planning Director, November 19, 1947, in the author's possession.

65. Shellhorn spent the weekend of December 4–5, 1948, in Santa Barbara, where she toured estate gardens by Lockwood de Forest and Ralph Stevens and the new University of California campus in Goleta. Shellhorn, ASLA files, in the author's possession.

66. Kevin Starr, "The Case Study House Program and the Impending Future: Some Regional Considerations," in *Blueprints for Modern Living: History and Legacy of the Case Study Houses,* ed. Elizabeth A. R. Smith, exhibition catalog (Los Angeles: Museum of Contemporary Art; Cambridge: MIT Press, 1989), 143; Reuben A. Rainey, "Organic Form in the Humanized Landscape: Garrett Eckbo's *Landscape for Living,*" in *Modern Landscape Architecure: A Critical Review,* ed. Marc Treib (Cambridge: MIT Press, 1993), 187.

67. Shellhorn, "Thoughts on Landscape Architecture," 1.

68. Shellhorn diaries, August 2, 1952.

69. Shellhorn, interview by author, November 17, 2004.

70. Shellhorn, interview by author, November 29, 2004.

71. Dorothy Chandler obituary, *New York Times,* July 8, 1997; Shellhorn, interview by author, November 17, 2004; Tony Breckenridge Niven to

Shellhorn, December 1979, box 24, folder 4, RSP; Adelaide Hixon to Shellhorn, March 1, 1976, box 18, folder 8, RSP.

72. Shellhorn, Pasadena Oral History interview, 66.

73. Shellhorn to Shirley Scott, March 7, 1955, box 373, folder 6, RSP.

74. All quotations in this and the following three paragraphs are from Shellhorn, "Thoughts on Landscape Architecture." Shellhorn wrote the essay to prepare for an interview with th,e *Los Angeles Examiner:* "How a Woman Feels about Landscaping," *Los Angeles Examiner,* April 16, 1961. Twenty years later she added the subtitle "Thoughts much the same in 1981, some thoughts added."

75. Dan Kaplanak Sr., telephone interview by author, April 26, 2011. Kaplanak was a young construction worker on the Fashion Square La Habra project when he met Shellhorn.

76. In 2011 Munger wrote, "It is not too much to say that my wife Nancy and I loved Ruth Shellhorn." Charles Munger, email to author, June 9, 2011.

77. "Shopping for Landscape Ideas," *Sunset Magazine,* March 1969, 96–101.

78. Shellhorn, interviews by author, November 3 and 29, 2004, and December 6, 2004.

79. Shellhorn diaries, June 14, 1949.

80. David C. Streatfield, conversation with author, April 15, 2011.

81. ASLA bulletin, Southern California chapter, September 1971, 1; *Western Landscaping News,* October 1971, 61.

82. The Bay Island Park commission came to Shellhorn through a referral from Nancy Munger. Shellhorn to Nancy Munger, February 2, 1988, box 3, folder 2, RSP.

83. Sam Hellinger, interview by author, June 10, 2011; Shellhorn, interview by author, December 6, 2004.

84. Harriet Doerr, "A Writer's Landscape," *Architectural Digest* 53 (November 1996): 63.

85. Alan Hess, remarks delivered at "Built by Becket: Centennial Celebration," Los Angeles, March 4, 2003; Shellhorn, interview by author, November 29, 2004; Louis Naidorf, interview by author, February 2007.

86. Shellhorn, interview by author, November 3, 2004.

87. Claire Noland, "Ruth Shellhorn, 97; Landscape Architect for Bullock's, Disneyland," *Los Angeles Times,* November 12, 2006.

SOUTH PASADENA HIGH SCHOOL

1. The Marsh and Russell firm also designed the beachfront town of Venice, California. The new Fine Arts and Science buildings were by Marsh, as the principal designer in the Marsh, Smith & Powell firm. See Jane Apostol, *South Pasadena: A Centennial History, 1888–1988* (South Pasadena, CA: South Pasadena Public Library, 1987), 50.

2. Ibid., 220; Sam Watters, email to author, January 19, 2014.

3. Shellhorn diaries, May 24, 1936.
4. Shellhorn, Pasadena Oral History interview, 34–35.
5. Shellhorn diaries, July 10, 1936.
6. Shellhorn, "Observations and Suggestions in regard to the Landscape Maintenance of the School Grounds," to South Pasadena Unified School District, October 13, 1938, in the author's possession; Shellhorn, Pasadena Oral History interview, 41.
7. The Art Court was the subject of an oil painting by Elizabeth Thurber, an art teacher at the high school, which was featured on the cover of the school yearbook in 1995. Mike Hogan, interview by author, January 14, 2014.
8. Belinda Bolterauer to Shellhorn, January 30, 2004, box 373, folder 11, RSP; Shellhorn, interview by author, December 6, 2004.

SHORELINE DEVELOPMENT STUDY

1. Shellhorn to Charles Bennet, City Planning Commission, February 10, 1943, in the author's possession.
2. Shellhorn, interview by author, November 17, 2004.
3. *Shoreline Development Study, Playa del Rey to Palos Verdes: A Portion of a Proposed Master Recreation Plan for the Greater Los Angeles Region* (Los Angeles: Greater Los Angeles Citizens Committee, 1944), 8–19. See also "Suggested Beach Highway System for an Eleven-Mile Shoreline Development," *Southwest Builder and Contractor,* July 1944, 20–27.
4. *Shoreline Development Study,* 28–33.
5. Shellhorn, interviews by author, November 17 and 29, 2004; Shellhorn to Monica Woolner, May 19, 1985, in the author's possession.
6. "Report on the Revised Master Plan of Shoreline Development," Los Angeles County Regional Planning Commission, February 1946.

BULLOCK'S PASADENA

1. Shellhorn, interviews by author, November 29, 2004, and June 1, 2006.
2. "An Introduction to Bullock's Pasadena," undated manuscript, Pasadena Museum of History archives; Pasadena Historical Society newsletter, September 1987, 1.
3. Shellhorn, interview by author, November 29, 2004.
4. Ibid.
5. Shellhorn to James J. Yoch, February 20, 1992, copy in the author's possession.
6. "Shopping Ease Featured in Store's Design," *Pasadena Star-News,* September 9, 1947.
7. Shellhorn, interview by author, November 17, 2004.

8. "An Introduction to Bullock's Pasadena."

9. Shellhorn, interview by author, June 6, 2006.

10. Shellhorn diaries, October 19, 1945.

11. "An Introduction to Bullock's Pasadena"; Shellhorn, interviews by author, November 17 and 29, 2004; Shellhorn, "Fashion Squares: Notes for Sunset Magazine," September 30, 1967, in the author's possession.

12. Shellhorn to Ben Rabe, February 6, 1950, copy in the author's possesion.

13. Shellhorn, interview by author, November 29, 2004.

14. Louis Naidorf, interview by author, February, 2007; "10 Years of Planning Culminated: Strikingly Designed Store Captures Spirit of Southland," *Pasadena Star-News,* September 9, 1947.

PRUDENTIAL INSURANCE COMPANY OF AMERICA, WESTERN HOME OFFICE

1. Shellhorn diaries, December 19, 1947. This may have been her first attempt to enlist Kueser, a skilled carpenter, in building a model.

2. Shellhorn, "Preliminary Landscape Plan for the Prudential Insurance Company of America," December 16, 1947, and "Landscape Plan for the Prudential Insurance Company of America," April 1948, both in box 131, folder 1, RSP.

3. Shellhorn diaries, February 5, 1948.

4. Shellhorn, "Preliminary Landscape Plan for the Prudential Insurance Company of America," and "Landscape Plan for the Prudential Insurance Company of America."

5. Shellhorn, "Landscape Plan for the Prudential Insurance Company of America."

6. American Association of Nurserymen to Shellhorn, November 26, 1954, copy in the author's possession.

KNAPP GARDEN

1. Quoted in James Brezina, "How a Woman Feels about Landscaping," *Los Angeles Examiner,* April 16, 1961.

2. "One Generous Patio for Entertaining . . . Another Secluded Patio for Privacy," *Sunset Magazine,* July 1955, 62–63.

3. Ibid.

4. "How Planting Can Soften the Rigid Lines of Garden Steps," *Sunset Magazine,* June 1954, 70; "These Garden Steps Invite You to Pause . . . Enjoy the Plants Nearby," *Sunset Magazine,* February 1956, 64–65.

5. Shellhorn diaries, May 27, 1953; and interview by author, November 29, 2004.

DISNEYLAND

1. Shellhorn, Pasadena Oral History interview, 62; and interview by author, November 17, 2004.
2. Shellhorn diaries, July 12, 1955.
3. The remaining acreage included service and parking areas and undeveloped areas set aside for expansion. Ruth Shellhorn, "Disneyland: Dream Built in One Year through Teamwork of Many Artists," *Landscape Architecture* 46 (April 1956): 132; Shellhorn, "Planting Plan for Front Entrance Showing Tree Planting," June 1, 1955, box 83, folder 1, RSP.
4. Shellhorn, "Disneyland," 124.
5. The concept of progressive realization, also known as "sequential viewing" or "concealment and revealment," was popularized by John Ormsbee Simonds in *Landscape Architecture: The Shaping of Man's Natural Environment* (New York: F. W. Dodge, 1961), 122.
6. Shellhorn, "Site Plan—Landscape Design & Tree Planting Plan—Hub Area," May 7, 1955, box 83, folder 1, RSP; Shellhorn, "Landscape Site Plan & Tree Planting Plan—Town Square," April 18, 1955, RSP.
7. Shellhorn, "Disneyland," 134; Shellhorn's "Disneyland" file, in the author's possession. Jack and Morgan Evans were descendants of a botanically inclined family; their father, Hugh Evans, cofounder of the Evans & Reeves nursery, was known as one of the "truly great plantsmen who have contributed to the advancement of horticulture in Southern California." His sons worked with him from the time they were boys and were hired by Walt Disney to help design Disneyland after landscaping his backyard railroad in the Holmby Hills section of Los Angeles. Victoria Padilla, *Southern California Gardens,* 89. Both brothers were "grandfathered in" when state licensing for landscape architects was enacted in California in 1954.
8. Shellhorn's "Disneyland" file, in the author's possession; Shellhorn, "Landscape Site Plan & Tree Planting Plan—Town Square"; Shellhorn, "Disneyland," 125.
9. Shellhorn, interview by author, November 17, 2004; Shellhorn diaries, May 24, 1955.
10. Shellhorn, "Disneyland," 127.
11. Disney was probably not involved in selecting Neuschwanstein specifically, but he approved the castle concept, which was then designed by the art directors.
12. "Disneyland—A Triumph in Landscaping," *Landscaping: The Magazine of Western Landscape Industry* 1 (August 1955): 8–10.
13. Morgan Evans, *Disneyland: World of Flowers* (Burbank: Walt Disney Productions, 1965), 15.
14. Shellhorn, "Disneyland," 127.
15. Shellhorn, "Landscape Design and Tree Planting Plan—Fantasyland," June 30, 1955, box 83, folder 1, RSP.

16. Shellhorn, "Disneyland," 135; Shellhorn, "Landscaping Fantasy Land—Landscape Design & Tree Planting Plan Showing Paving Lay-out," June 30, 1955, box 83, folder 1, RSP.

17. Shellhorn's "Disneyland" file.

18. Shellhorn, "Landscaping Frontierland and Adventureland—Landscape Design & Tree Planting Plan—Central Areas," May 23, 1955, box 83, folder 1, RSP, and "Disneyland" file.

19. Shellhorn, "Disneyland," 131; Shellhorn, "Site Plan—Landscape Design & Tree Planting Plan—Hub Area," May 7, 1955, box 83, folder 1, RSP; pencil revisions on "Revised Landscape Design & Tree Planting Plan—Hub Area," June 18, 1955, in the author's possession.

20. Shellhorn, "Landscape Design and Tree Planting Plan, Showing Paving Layout [for Tomorrowland]," June 25, 1955, box 83, folder 1, RSP.

21. Shellhorn's plan specified only "color" for this area. Morgan Evans describes this specific planting scheme in *Disneyland: World of Flowers,* 23.

22. Shellhorn, "Landscape Design & Tree Planting Plan—Central Areas," June 8, 1955, box 83, folder 1, RSP.

23. While acknowledging that it was impossible to give credit to all the people who contributed to the landscape design of Disneyland, Walt Disney singled out Shellhorn in the preface to Morgan Evans's *Disneyland: World of Flowers*: "Special plaudits are due to Ruth Patricia Shellhorn for her design of the formal Victorian plan for Main Street, the Town Square and the Plaza." He further complimented her astute selection of trees and shrubs, which gave such character to the park.

UNIVERSITY OF CALIFORNIA, RIVERSIDE

1. "University of California, Riverside Campus: Timeline," www.ucr.edu/about/timeline.html.

2. Shellhorn, "Landscaping," in the "Campus Environment" section of George Vernon Russell F.A.I.A. & Associates, *Long Range Development Plan, University of California, Riverside*, May 1964, 12–17, in the author's possession.

3. A nearly identical land use issue arose in the 1940s and early 1950s at the University of California at Los Angeles and resulted in the filling of an eighty-five-foot deep ravine that intersected the campus. "Half a Century as a Southern California Landscape Architect," Oral History Program, University of California, Los Angeles, 1970 (interview of Ralph D. Cornell conducted by Enid H. Douglass in 1967), 223–25.

4. Russell & Associates, *Long Range Development Plan*, 15.

5. Shellhorn to R. J. Evans, Chief Architect, May 11, 1961, box 28, folder 10, RSP. Shellhorn sometimes referred to the Health Sciences building as the Health Services building.

6. Russell & Associates, *Long Range Development Plan*, 13. The plan in-

cluded Shellhorn's "South Campus Landscape Plan" and "Entrance Mall Landscape Plan."

7. Shellhorn, interview by author, November 29, 2004; Dawn Bonker, email to author, September 12, 2005.

8. Foreword, Russell & Associates, *Long Range Development Plan,* v.

9. Shellhorn's residential commissions would continue to increase, and twenty years later Russell would hire her to design landscapes for his homes in Pasadena (1984) and South Pasadena (1988).

BULLOCK'S FASHION SQUARE SHOPPING CENTERS

1. "Bullock's Plans $14 Million New 'Environment Control,'" *Los Angeles Times,* April 30, 1967; Richard Longstreth, *City Center to Regional Mall: Architecture, the Automobile, and Retailing in Los Angeles, 1920–1950* (Cambridge: MIT Press, 1998), 344–47.

2. Longstreth, *City Center to Regional Mall,* 344–47.

3. "Santa Ana Has Beautiful New Fashion Square," *Southwest Builder and Contractor,* August 22, 1958, 6–8. See also *Los Angeles Times* advertising supplement, March 14, 1968; "Bullock's Plans $14 Million New 'Environment Control'"; and "Bullock's Santa Ana to Be Sixth in Southland Retailing 'Family'" and "Fashion Square Fact Sheet," Bullock's press releases, September 16, 1958, in the author's possession.

4. Shellhorn, interviews by author, November 3 and 29, 2004.

5. Quoted in "Santa Ana Has Beautiful New Fashion Square," 8.

6. *Los Angeles Times* advertising supplement, 8.

7. Quoted in "A Study of Ruth Patricia Shellhorn, Award Winning Landscape Architect," *Landscape Design and Construction* 13 (October 1967): 8–9.

8. Ibid., 3. See also Shellhorn, interview by author, November 29, 2004.

9. Shellhorn, interview by author, November 29, 2004.

10. "Fashion Square Landscape Plan Creates Garden-like Effect," Bullock's press release, September 16, 1958, in the author's possession.

11. "A Study of Ruth Patricia Shellhorn," 15–16.

12. Ibid. See also Bullock's Santa Ana Landscape Planting Plan, Sheet 1, June 1958, box 135, folder 1, RSP.

13. "A Study of Ruth Patricia Shellhorn," 14.

14. Ibid., 11.

15. Ibid., 21.

16. Melinda Wood, comments to the author, October 16, 2010; Robert M. Fletcher, videotaped lecture, February 19, 1994, California State Polytechnic University, Pomona, Library of Environmental Design.

17. Shellhorn, interview by author, November 29, 2004.

18. Ibid.

19. Ibid.

20. Erik Katzmaier, interview by author, March 2011; correspondence between Shellhorn and Ann Zemer, March 1982, Miscellaneous Correspondence file, in the author's possession.
21. "Shopping for Landscape Ideas," *Sunset Magazine,* March 1969, 96–101.
22. Shellhorn, interview by author, November 29, 2004.
23. Awards included a "100%" rating from the Santa Ana Chamber of Commerce Civic Beautification Award Committee in 1966; a Daisy award from the California Landscape Contractors Association in 1970; an Environmental Improvement award from the Associated Landscape Contractors of America in 1981; and the Landscape Architecture Award of Merit by the California Garden Clubs, Inc., in 1984.
24. Shellhorn, interview by author, November 29, 2004.

MARLBOROUGH SCHOOL

1. According to Shellhorn, Nancy Munger questioned the capability of the school's landscape architect, Robert Herrick Carter, after he supposedly created a plan with camellias located in direct sunlight. Shellhorn, interview by author, March 21, 2006. Carter, however, was not only one of the earliest registered landscape architects in California but also an accomplished plantsman with a thriving maintenance business. He and Shellhorn worked together as members of Landscape Architects 4 Los Angeles, a professional committee, in 1983.
2. Shellhorn, "Library Court Paving Plan & Tree Well Detail," April 19, 1967, box 54, folder 2, RSP.
3. Shellhorn, "Landscape and Planting Plan," September 1981, box 54, folder 2, RSP.
4. Shellhorn, "Suggested Alternate Plan for Flagpole Area," April 25, 1967, box 54, folder 2, RSP.
5. The cranes were cast in Naples, Italy, from an artist's mold. Peter Chinnici, archivist, Marlborough School, email to author, March 24, 2014.
6. Shellhorn, "Design Plan for Senior Garden," May 18, 1967, box 54, folder 2, RSP.

HIXON GARDEN

1. Thornton Ladd was the original architect for both the first and the second houses. The project architect for the Jones remodel was William Pelkus.
2. Hannah Carter, Nancy Munger, and Ann Mudd were part of the network of influential Los Angeles women who commissioned work from Shellhorn and recommended her to many others. Shellhorn met Edward Carter through Welton Becket in 1956 and designed two resi-

dential gardens for him, the second for him and his wife, Hannah, in Bel-Air in 1965. Hannah Carter recommended Shellhorn to Ann and Henry T. Mudd in the early 1970s, and the 1975 Hixon commission came from both the Mudds. Henry was the son of Harvey Mudd, benefactor of Harvey Mudd College in Claremont.

3. Shellhorn, interview by author, November 3, 2004.
4. Shellhorn, "General Landscape Plan—Motor Court Area," March 1, 1976, box 160, folder 1, RSP.
5. Shellhorn's notes, planting lists, and specifications, box 18, folder 9, RSP.
6. Shellhorn, travel journal, June 21–July 2, 1933, in the author's possession.

BRACKENRIDGE / NIVEN GARDEN

1. Shellhorn's project index, 1935–1988, box 361, RSP; and Fran Neuman (Tony's daughter), email correspondence with author, November 12–28, 2006.
2. This residence was one of Van Pelt's first commissions after leaving his partnership with the Pasadena architects Sylvanus Marston and Edger Maybury. Van Pelt traveled extensively in Europe and in Mexico and wrote *Old Architecture in Southern Mexico* (1926). Ann Scheid Lund, *Historic Pasadena: An Illustrated History* (San Antonio, TX: Historical Publishing Network, 1999), 110; Kathleen Tuttle, *Sylvanus Marston: Pasadena's Quintessential Architect* (Santa Monica, CA: Hennessey and Ingalls, 2001), 6–7, 74.
3. Robert M. Fletcher, videotaped lecture, February 19, 1994, California State Polytechnic University, Pomona, Library of Environmental Design.
4. Fran Neuman, telephone conversation with author, November 28, 2006.
5. Shellhorn, "General Landscape Plan of Rear Garden," January 26, 1979, box 152, folder 1, RSP.
6. Tony Brackenridge Niven to Ruth Shellhorn, December, 1979, box 24, folder 4, RSP.

DOERR GARDEN

1. Yoch was preparing to retire in Carmel, California. In addition to the Doerr garden, the projects Shellhorn acquired included a garden for Scribner Birlenbach in West Los Angeles (1950) and, in Pasadena, gardens for Mr. and Mrs. Lawrence Brooks (1951) and Mr. and Mrs. Richard Call (1979). Tony Brackenridge recommended her for the Call commission and Ann Mudd for the Doerr garden.

2. Ann Scheid Lund, *Historic Pasadena: An Illustrated History* (San Antonio, TX: Historical Publishing Network, 1999); James J. Yoch, *Landscaping the American Dream* (New York: Abrams, 1989), 51–54.

3. Lund, *Historic Pasadena,* 124; Yoch, *Landscaping the American Dream,* 51 (quotation).

4. Yoch, *Landscaping the American Dream,* 51–54.

5. See notes in Shellhorn's project index, 1935–1988, box 361, RSP.

6. Shellhorn to James Yoch, May 2, 1988, in the author's possession.

7. Shellhorn, interview by author, December 16, 2004.

8. Pasadena Heritage Oral History Project, "Interview with Ruth Patricia Shellhorn," conducted by Molly Johnson (Pasadena: Pasadena Oral History Project, 2002), 42.

9. Harriet Doerr, "A Writer's Landscape," *Architectural Digest* 53 (November 1996): 54–58, 63.

INDEX

Page numbers in *italics* refer to illustrations.